Coffee on the Rocks

Resa Milan

Vortext, LLC

Vortex: any activity, situation or way of life regarded as irresistibly engulfing

Acknowledgements

The team that assisted in the process that created **Coffee on the Rocks** and the companion **Cookbook** was the greatest on Earth. Thanks to my lovely and talented daughter, Genevieve Barker, whose curiosity and appetite first made the initial request for the original recipes from the **Weathervane Café.** My family supported my endeavors with assistance, patience, and encouragement: many thanks to Aaron, Susan, and Alexandria. My sisters, Patricia Moffitt and Susan Keegan lent their typing and transcription skills, and my nieces, Amy, Julia, and Ashley added editing and advice. I want to thank performing comedian, Pete Christensen, for his humor and assurance that the laughs would come on their own. A huge thanks goes to Lawrence Schreiber for all the organization and record keeping. Mike Burdick kept the computer in fine tune and assisted with cover art, music and God-given talent. And finally, a huge round of applause is sent to Sedona's own Tom Bird and his method of bringing the writing out with his unique methods using immersion into a Sedona experience and the *TomBirdSeminars.com*.

Coffee on the Rocks

By Resa Milan

Published by Vortext, LLC

CoffeeontheRockstheNovel.com

Cover Design by Mike Burdick

cedarwinds0310@yahoo.com

Layout by Launchpad Press, Cody, WY

www.launchpad-press.com

ISBN-13: 978-0-9838655-0-6

Contents

Chapter 1

BURSTING THROUGH THE GLASS doors of the medical clinic after a day's work was not an ending but rather a frantic beginning of another career. I stooped to perform a rapid change of clothes in the Bessemer furnace-like heat of the parking lot, crouched behind my car door. Even with no one in sight, I felt the creepy tingling feeling that eyes were on me and chalked it up to the energy fields of the Sedona Vortex. As I squirmed out of the lab coat and scrubs, I heard a strange whooshing roar followed by raucous giggling and the chattering clicks of camera shutters. With my new monogrammed coffee shop polo shirt bunched around my neck and my lingerie exposed, I felt the shadow of a hot-air balloon float slowly over my head. The balloon was filled with tourists. They got an eyeful and I hid my red face against the car. I couldn't worry about strangers; I needed to get inside the coffee shop—my brand new baby—and work the afternoon shift.

The blinding Arizona sun was as high as the temperature that late July afternoon and the new artsy coffee shop sign was glinting with a thousand dollars of fourteen-carat gold paint. Wafts of hot, dry, dusty air swirled around the car tires and my ankles. A dust devil skittered across the parking lot rearranging small stones. The eucalyptus trees dangled long lengths of branches on the light wind causing the arid, fragrant leaves that gently perfumed the air to sway in pearl gray curtains. Everything was toasting in the heat: the foliage a pale silvery-green, the earth a crunchy brown and the vistas colored in red rock crimson.

Sliding on loose gravel with my heartbeat thumping in my ears, I made a mad dash to the all-consuming project I had thrown myself into, the Weathervane Café, my Sedona coffee shop.

The glimmer and sparkle of the pale grape sign rimmed in genuine gold reflected my optimism at attempting this fledgling enterprise. My hurry to get into the Weathervane Café was brisk in spite of the eight hour shift I just completed. My medical job's weekly salary rapidly drained into this startup business. To date, I was the sole investor. It was up to me to make it…or it could break me.

The soft opening had been a week ago and the fresh paint smell was just fading away. Once again, I allowed myself a second of admiration over my choice of colors. I could feel the mixture of pride, excitement, and fear well up in my throat as I looked overhead at the glistening sign with my logo. The backs of my hands were tingling with pinpricks of tension and my mind was already on the daunting list of tasks before me.

The stunning transformation still made me pause and pull in a long breath as I admired the change. The remodeled coffee shop walls were now an understated shade of light lavender with gold accents. A deep purple industrial vinyl featuring a perfectly centered, four-pointed star replaced the filthy green indoor-outdoor carpeting, the first item to be scraped up and rolled out, worn by years of traffic and spills. The new design and original artwork hanging on the walls had transformed a shabby, rundown sandwich shop with the style of a New Jersey bus terminal into my personal vision of a civilized eatery.

By this time of the day, my stomach was rumbling as I smelled the leftover aromas from the lunch business. After all the months of planning, I created a fresh theme and took pride and joy in my menu. My primary goal was to add a regional Southwest zing, a new direction in taste, using the neglected desert flavors of mesquite, Manzanita, cactus, jojoba and juniper. My recipes were new and original.

The menu expressed that wish. I had deliberated long hours over a balance of freshly prepared selections that had a homemade taste and zesty desert flavors. The taste was a commingling of Native American tribal foods, the Hispanic influences of Mexico with a generous measure of Santa Fe stews simmered with New Mexico's finest Hatch chilies. There were a dozen opportunities on the menu to sample cactus in all its forms—from the tangy, lemony, green bean flavor in the napalitos salad to the luscious fruit of the prickly pear, edible cactus was a highlighted and featured item. My favorite was a silky, sweetly tart dressing with a hot pink color; it laced the baby spinach salad, textured with ripe strawberries and crunchy sliced pecans. Even the lemonade was a shade of bright magenta accenting the cactus's unusual flavor.

After canvassing the Sedona restaurants as a customer for a number of years and interrogating a resident food expert and former chef named Roland, I originated a phrase that defined the style of my cuisine: *"Sedona Ranch."* The concept came to me by imagining what my future customer would want: *After hours on horseback dreamily lost among the red-rock scenery, lungs pumped on cold, fresh air, a person craves hearty ranch-hand fare.*

The phrase defined my new enterprise and my mission statement appeared at the bottom and back of the gold colored menu cards.

Our style is innovative and called
"Sedona Ranch,"
Using regional ingredients and recipes
Featuring long-time favorites.

Whenever I considered a meal out, I searched for an elusive trio of standards: the ethnic, soul touched flavor of the dish, the appropriate background music, and a quiet private alcove.

Here at my new coffee shop, which was growing into a café, music ranged from Sinatra to Sting, from big band to jazz. Everything was up-tempo and nothing disharmonious was allowed. The background music would blend and complement the customer's digestion; the food would be deliciously created with care and a visual feast would greet the patrons. The stage was set. The Weathervane Café would be a hit!

The four million tourists visiting annually wanted a Southwestern experience they could taste to accompany the adventure, spiritualism, and soul-stirring scenery that sets Sedona apart in domestic and international vacation destinations.

Hurrying across the patio, I glanced skyward giving the original artwork on the glossy new sign a prideful glance. The coffee shop's sign featured the design of a weathervane, one that could be hammered into metal and placed atop a roof. I had purchased it from a talented artist, Gerry Hoover, a friend for years until his passing. I was a minor collector of his work. The image was a spectacular representation of a man, woman, and horse or more precisely a half-horse. The man reined the magnificently breast-plated steed through space and balanced the woman on his left hand at the level of her heart. The two figures in the image were nude; maybe

Hoover intended them to represent Adam and Eve. The image became my logo, branding the new business. The original drawing was framed and displayed prominently on the coffee shop's wall.

As I strode into the coffee shop, I was mentally ticking off the visible problems seeing my lavender dream diluted with realities: employee cars parked in prime customer spots, trash cans overflowing from the lunch rush, tables littered, newly planted flowers wilting in the July heat, wind swept debris on the patio floor, handprints on the double glass doors leading into the entrance, music blaring too loudly, and misspelled words on the blackboard that displayed the daily specials. As I crossed the threshold, anxiety mingled with high hopes and I shivered in spite of the heat and tried to ignore the rumbles in my gut.

Adrenaline was running rampant in my veins and arteries but obviously not in my small staff of food assemblers and waiters. The contrast between us made me aware of the buzzing in my ears that was pure raw energy. The workers had wound down after the lunch rush and were looking forward to leaving as soon as possible. Dirty lunch dishes were piled shoulder high in the sink room. Tomorrow's food prep had not even begun. As I eyeballed the scene, I felt my nostrils flare. My next shift was about to begin, but first I needed a coffee or an iced tea or whatever caffeinated beverage I could grab and I needed it now!

Immediately, my general manager, Barry, confronted me. Barry possessed a combination of charm, disarming looks, proper manners, and intelligence but most of all a talkativeness that spotlighted his humor. That was on the surface. Beneath that facade was a wisecracking, irreverent wit that worshipped old Don Rickles' comedy routines. His conversations were punctuated with antics from the Three Stooges doctored with his own personal twist. In truth, Barry was never silent. If he wasn't doing a Curly-like "whoop-whoop-whoop" at a red light then he was chattering on about the latest gossip and news. Just how much and long he could talk in a twenty-four hour period was yet to be revealed to me. After all, we had been busy working full-time jobs while making plans and preparations for this business endeavor for the last five months.

His eyes locked onto mine. He had a laundry list of grumbles behind the look. He was harassed and more than a little annoyed.

"How's the film business, Miss Harlow? In his eternal stand-up comic routine, he was referring to my occupation as an X-ray technologist. "I've got some questions and like it or not, you're the one with all the answers," he growled, as he flicked invisible cigar ashes and raised his eyebrows *ala* Groucho Marks.

He always teased me with silly flirtatious nicknames. Harmless enough, but I realized this was his way of defusing the attraction he felt for me. I'd worked around enough men in my life to recognize genuine interest from sexist remarks or some type of outright come-on. There wasn't a mutual attraction. I was too busy to think about romance with anyone, least of all a man ten years younger and a business partner in this new venture.

"Same as always; the three M's. An MVA, mayhem, and murder," I answered.

"Just as I suspected," he said.

Before he could go on, I pointed to the menu chalkboard. "I see we're serving 'Butter Nut Squashed Soup' and 'Hatched Green Chilies.' Which one of our employees wrote that?"

Still in Groucho mode, Barry responded, "The most intelligent employee, of course."

He pointed a finger across the room to lay the guilt on Gerry who spoke the best English of anyone on the crew.

"Squashed and hatched sound like an accident to me," I said.

"You would know," he said.

I tossed him a damp cloth lying next to the cash register. "Rub that out and make the correction, will you? People won't trust us to put the right ingredients in the dishes if we can't even spell them."

"You're every wish is my reprimand, *El Commandante,*" he answered with a mock salute.

"So any updates, Barry?" I asked. "How's everything going?"

"Just a couple of comments," he answered.

"Oh, what?" I asked.

"'The cilantro was too stemmy and the peas in the Chicken Wild Rice Soup were canned,'" he reported.

"Too stemmy?" I repeated.

"Yeah."

"The peas are never canned," I said.

"I know, I know, but the customer said with great authority that she was a grad of the *Le Cordon Bleu*," he said.

"So what did you do," I asked. Again, the inner doubts of whether I could make the change from healthcare professional to business owner, to pay the bills and make a living rippled through me. Looming was the dark shape of a shore-hugging shark flashing near a naïve, dog-paddling swimmer.

"Just what you would do…I sent them a free dessert and gave my deepest sympathies to her husband," Barry said.

"Atta, boy!"

I rolled my eyes and made sure he saw it, but when I turned away I smiled to myself. He may be a little crazy, but sometimes a little crazy is just what's needed to get through the constant pressure of a never-ending workweek.

Barry was bobbing and weaving behind my back and around my ears as I shoved my bag on a shelf in an out-of-the-way spot. The rack was ceiling-high, stainless steel shelving, holding the supplies needed on a daily basis. I was really in the mood for a stiff cold drink, a shower, and a long break in a recliner. I turned to discover Barry back in my face.

"You've got to let me know, you got to write it down… what's in the soup?" he questioned.

"Why?" I asked, wrinkling my forehead in a dismissive smirk. "Now you want me to reel off the ingredients? I'm too tired to think, let alone talk."

"It's the lunch customers and the Tin Foil Hat Lady," he explained. "One can't have dairy, the next one is allergic to wheat. Then somebody is off sugar and every other one is not eating meat or anything with a meat broth. Soooo, yes, you little Soup Shieska, what's in the pot?"

"I'll never tell. Who the hell is the Tin Foil Hat Lady?"

"Honest to goodness, today a lady came in wearing a hat and before she ordered she asked, 'That's a microwave over there, isn't it?'" he began to explain. "So, I answered, 'Yes, ma'am it is.' She tipped the hat she was wearing and low and behold, it was lined with aluminum foil. 'Young man, don't use that contraption on anything I order!' I'm serious, she had so much metal on her head, she turned south and we picked up a radio station in Phoenix."

"Invite her back on Sunday. We'll serve hot dogs and beer and the foil hat can broadcast the game."

"Oooh, you're sexy when you're talking sports to me. I think I like that."

"We've got work to do. I can hear your fairy tales later," I said.

"I'm telling you, this woman actually wears tin foil in her hat. She told me we should all wear hats with tin foil to protect us from the rays," he explained.

"Rays?"

"Yeah, gamma rays, beta rays, sting rays, Tampa Bay Rays. Who knows what's on the list?"

"That last one's a baseball team," I pointed out.

"Okay, so I embellished a bit, just the same, you get my point. She warned me about the Vortex and dirty electricity, too."

"I've heard about that, the energy spirals, right, but what is dirty electricity?"

Not one to pass up a punch line, Barry instantly transformed into sci-fi writer Rod Sterling. He stood erect with his hands clasped in front of him in his best *Twilight Zone* pose. "The Vortex is a massive aura of undetected evil energy ready to engulf and devour all those unsuspecting innocent victims who unwittingly dare to enter its dark, non-caring clutches."

"Oh, like a mortgage company?"

"Exactly," he answered.

"Okay, let's get some work done," I was a bit irritated already, feeling belligerent after eight hard hours on my feet. While Barry wanted to play, my job was to work and worry.

"You've got to write it down," he pleaded. "I've had questions all day, so what's in the soup? I mean the two soups?"

"I'm not telling. That's my little secret." I fluffed off into the sink room.

The menu always carried at least two soups, since I love making soup following the classic recipes. Our menu offered a bowl and a roll for $5.50. Often, however, I orchestrated an original and healthy concoction, for I believe that soup is the perfect food, not milk.

"Catch me later! It looks like there's an hour of clean up before I can even start on the new batches of salad dressings." I wavered between sheer nervous energy and frustration.

"Oh, by the way," he informed me, "We're already out of the prickly pear cream cheese, the green chili posole and your sweet pea soup."

"Then get in here!" I was armoring myself with our monogrammed apron as I started the massive organization of layer upon layer of dirty dishes; the randomly stacked bowls and glasses. None had been scraped or sorted into uniform piles and the unfinished bits, melted ice cubes and garnishes had to be discarded first.

"Barry," I said, "There's a four letter word I want you to remember."

"Lust, kiss, urge, itch, heat, sexy, stud… romp?" he asked.

"No, S-O-R-T, sort," I answered as I waved my hand at the mess in the sink. "Make sure this is cleaned up before I get here from now on."

"Yes, boss."

The big commercial dishwasher did not work like a home model and our service representative came in every other day making adjustments. The cycle took about ten minutes and sounded like a tornado bearing down. It was deafening. Dishes, glassware and silverware came out washed and rinsed.

"I'll load and wash, you dry and put away. This monster sends the dishes back hot and wet," I said.

Right on cue Barry whispered in my ear, "Now that is a condition I can cure, from hot and wet to relaxed and happy."

"Back to work!"

"I have some other things to tell you," Barry said.

I moaned. I didn't want to listen to anything in the chamber of rushing water sounds, the clanks from old plumbing, and a roaring dishwasher motor.

Already, after three weeks of formal ownership, I was ready to duck and cover. A week's vacation on a deserted beach with a lounge chair and a good book should have been the logical interlude between the start-up and the grand opening. There would be no luxury of a rest. Once the clock started on the monthly rent, it was up to me to get the cash register ringing.

The initial remodel, burying the shabby gray look, took two weeks due to a heavy and meticulously planned construction schedule. The success of that project was due to some excellent planning and a bulky, tattooed female carpenter named Nancy, who had a string of unconventional assistants. They looked like former inmates, recently released "timers."

The three workers spoke only to Nancy and not at all to Barry or me. Grizzled, semi-toothless, and garbed in tissue-paper-thin, discarded hand-me-downs, the helpers were neither showered nor cologned. They were, however, as reliable as an old Timex watch and worked at a steady tick-tock pace, so focused on each task that their eyes looked far into the future, their ears dumbed down to the sounds around them.

Nancy was the big-boned gal from a *k.d. Lang* song lyric. The local restaurant equipment representative, Ed, who sang her praises as honest, dependable, and steadfast had recommended her. These were highly regarded traits for any carpenter: to come in on schedule, on budget, and complete the job.

I met Nancy on a quick half- hour lunch break. She agreed to meet me at the back door of the medical clinic and as we sat at an outdoor table, I gobbled a sandwich and sketched out a design for the planned retail alcove. It was simple and practical with lower cabinets to hide back inventory and a progression of shelving above to show off the items for sale: the gifts, gadgets, and goodies. The back wall would contain the modular display for hanging the kitchen tools. Nancy got the design in her mind at first glance at my penciled drawing and went to work. The finished nook was a shopping mini-mall of tourist take home treasures.

Barry was still behind my head, "Resa, I have a lot of details to go over."

"You can tell me while we clean up." I started complaining under my breath. As Barry looked for a towel, the sound track of Curley, Moe, and Shemp leaked from his lips: "NUC, NUC, NUC!"

"Until we get this mess cleaned up, I can't start making the items for tomorrow and I won't get home until 9:00 tonight…even later," I grouched.

"Yeah, yeah, I know. They're building the statue of

you next to Saint Theresa right now," he shot.

"Then up again at 6:00AM tomorrow to start all over again and now they want me to commit to the night call schedule at the medical clinic," I whined.

I was furiously cleaning, making a tub of bleach water to soak wipe-down cloths, scraping garbage, and sorting silverware from crockery and glassware while we talked.

"Well," he chuckled, "First, a couple of white people in Indian robes came in here today and wanted to talk to you."

"About what? What kind of Indian?" This was not a silly question as we were in Sedona, located near the reservations inhabited by a number of Native American tribes. The place abounded with the Navajo, Pima, and Apache.

"White people, you say?" I was confused.

"Yeah, seems like they met at an ashram in India while meditating and both took on Indian names. They're now calling themselves Dipti and Ranjit. I kept calling them Dippy and Ramjet, but I don't think they noticed."

I was cranking the dishwasher as fast as I could, sliding the steaming hot racks in and out. Actually, the ancient beast frightened me.

Barry was hopelessly slow at the drying; his expertise was all in the mouth. Talking was his forte. His strongest quality was his ability to remember the minutia of the day and to bark out orders. Accomplishing tasks that involved his hands, arms, or back was something he avoided. He was still a boy at heart, one who still used a lava lamp

15

as a nightlight. At home, he maintained a shrine to his sainted comedians, vestiges of the 1930's and 1940's, in the form of a display of refrigerator magnets. Twelve images of the Stooges were on shiny metal cameos: a gallery of adoration.

The next god that Barry worshipped was the coffee bean. A corner nook was covered with a dusky, granular yard of burlap from a Central American coffee bag. It served as an altar cloth to honor his religious practice of the brew. Instead of a chalice and cross, his various tools to grind, tamp, and measure were on display. Worship was conducted around the varieties vaulted in his freezer which contained carefully labeled, airtight, freshly roasted, expensive, estate grown selections. These bags arrived from a small private roaster within hours of the first or second crack, labeled with magnificent descriptions of the undertones of flavor: *a dusting of vanilla with a subtle hazelnut bite follows an exotic spice finish that walks on velvet slippers.*

The bags and jars, hermetically sealed, dominated his freezer and were stacked like logs of cordwood, patiently waiting to meet the boiling water and the ignition point of the flavor's release.

My head was shaking in disbelief. "So, what'd they want, these wanna be Indians?"

"They have a licensed home bakery and want to sell you their products. I think it might be a good idea."

"So what exactly *is* the product?" I asked.

"Sugarless cakes, individually wrapped," he said.

"And the good idea is…?

"Cause if it doesn't sell within three days, they take it back and we don't pay. We only pay for what we sell." He reeled off the economics.

"So what happens to the leftovers?" I asked.

Barry just shrugged. The question of the recycling of Dipti's sugarless cakes just hung there.

Chapter 2

ACTUALLY, I COULDN'T EVEN grasp the concept of taking on a new supplier, whether it was sugarless or not with the roar of the dishwasher and Barry yammering in my ear. I needed some peace and quiet and caffeine. That was obtainable, since as we had coffee, great coffee! It rivaled the new big name in coffee, only ours wasn't overly roasted or burned. For the past months, several coffee vendors, competing for our business, courted us by layering on samples of free beans. Lately, I had tasted a bevy of coffee from around the world. I was considering supply, price, and availability. There were a series of coffee cuppings accompanied by slurping sounds and much serious discussion about the mouth-feel, the texture, and the aftertaste of the many varieties that we tried. In contrast to a wine tasting with the savoring gargle, we spooned and munched the brews searching for tones of ripe fruit, chocolate, and balance.

The Celebes, excellent on body and balance, were just too pricey. Tanzania Peaberry gave off aromas of butter and honey with soft, multi-dimensional notes but the supply could be undependable. Finally, an Ethiopian Harrar, complex, bold and promising a blackberry hint became the favorite. We searched for an espresso that created a thick *crèma* like the foam on a stormy ocean and contained the sweetness of the jasmine-scented coffee blossoms from which it had sprung a year earlier.

Due to the generosity and coffee obsession of our local coffee representative, Ron Everett, who courted us with many varieties and blends, we accumulated a private stash to either hoard or offer as a special. Barry and I had a sideline hobby of seeking that special cup of "Joe" with a syrupy, earthy-wet, Irish moss flavor, intensely aromatic with low acid and spiciness. This love of the noble brew was a bond we shared. We sought coffees with a bright and tangy toast flavor. Our taste buds searched for the nectar to make us salivate shamelessly like a St. Bernard hound. Our noses picked up roasted walnuts and forest mushrooms when we were at the grinding station. And like all connoisseurs, we learned that the catty and sulfur notes promised a thrilling chemical change with the addition of boiling water. We stashed the pure Kona and Costa Rican for our private Sunday morning business meetings. All other coffee, other than what we poured at the shop, tasted like rags boiled in dishwater.

We had been tweaking the temperature settings, the grind and the varieties to get that perfect shot of "Joe" and we were both learning the intricacies of our commercial espresso machines, the twin *La Pavonis*. Barry was way ahead of any of the staff on the subject of coffee. He had an in-depth experience from a former long stint at the Plantation Company and was teaching our newbies, some rough inexperienced kids, how to assemble drinks and decorate the *crèma* in waves of hearts, fans, and flowers. Down deep he was both a barista and a coffee *affezionato*.

Our coffee representative, Ron Everett, from Seattle's Best, explained how the bean prices fluctuated on the world markets and where the action took place in Hong Kong, South America and Africa. The green bean prices would vary wildly according to the weather conditions, labor force, and political climate of the coffee producing countries. We were ensured a stable wholesale, roasted whole bean price of $5.25 a pound by entering into a six-month renewable contract with his company. Knowing that the bean price was fixed made calculating a major part of the monthly budget manageable. As Ron had pointed out, I needed to be aware of the best quality beans at the lowest price or else my main commodity could put my monthly budget beyond reach. That was just one more worry on my shoulders in the unfathomable adventure of new business ownership.

"I could kill for a good coffee," I warned. "Go make me one."

"OK, Doll Face, what'll it be today?" He was now dismissed on a fun errand and could put down the dishcloth.

"My favorite, a caramel *macchiato*, a double, no, today make it a triple, with an extra squirt of syrup over ice." I was taking a grave risk of dying of tachycardia in the late afternoon while furiously cleaning up after a loose staff of green kids. "And tomorrow, make sure these dishes are out of the way before I get here," I growled.

"Sir, yes Sir!" he answered, clicking his heels together, mocking me in a goofy way, always the one for foolery. At least I didn't have to endure a knuckle crunching "Moe" sound or the wave of a "Curley" hand gesture under my nose as he exited. He was glad to be free of the sink room.

It was now past 5:30 PM and the staff was marching out the day's trash, splitting up tips, mopping the floor with groans, and hurrying to do the 'Close.' We weren't equipped yet to serve dinners; our hours were 6:00 AM to 6:00 PM.

As I looked over the expanse of the coffee shop's dining area, I reminisced over the change in my trio of servers, the Filipino brothers, Gordon, Gerry, and Grant. The transformation of their appearance and skills from that first day's meeting was a remarkable contrast. The week before the opening, Barry and I were getting excited about our first operational day. He was busy doing some touch-ups with paintbrush in hand. I was on my knees washing the inside of an under-counter refrigerator.

"I can't wait to get the place open," he said.

"Yeah, so far it's all out-go into the bottomless pit without a dime coming in," I replied.

"I could buy some gum or mints on the installment plan."

"Don't complain," I answered. "I could wallpaper this place with all the checks I've written so far."

"You're like the French army. All you do is withdraw," he remarked.

"Very funny. Save that for one of your open mike nights. You'll get groans from other people besides me." As I rose and stretched my back, I saw three brown faces smiling through the big glass doors, hands shielding their eyes, their noses pressed to the front door.

"We've got visitors," I said. "Maybe they think we're open."

As I waved them in, all three waved in unison and they moved one step at a time as a unit. Then as they entered the coffee shop, they almost fell over one another.

"What can we do for you guys?" Barry asked.

The tallest announced in a heavy Tagalog accent, "I am Gordon and these are my brothers, Gerry and Grant."

"Betcha all the rest of the family has "G" names, too," mocked Barry, as he offered a paint-speckled handshake. Barry went round robin, including me in the introductions and handshakes.

Gordon piped up, "I am looking for a place for my artwork. Is this place up for rent?" In Vanna White style, he gestured to his brothers who pulled up shirts to reveal their tattooed chests. Like trained acrobats in a circus act they spun around to show off their backs as billboards to Gordon's art.

"You guys are really into tattoos," Barry gasped.

"No, but I had to practice on someone," replied Gordon.

"You want to see more?" Gordon asked. The other two scrambled with pant legs and belt buckles.

"Halt, easy there, boys. We're selling soups, sandwiches and coffees not beefcake and ink," Barry said. All three smiled innocently.

"So, can we work here?" asked Gordon.

"Impossible for a tattoo parlor, but yes to manual labor," I answered.

"Excuse us for just a moment," said Barry. "You boys amuse yourselves while we talk. Go ahead and check each other's green cards. We'll be back before you can say '*La Migra*.'"

Barry put an arm over my shoulder. We turned our backs to them and stepped just a few feet away.

Barry whispered, "Are you seriously thinking of hiring the G-men?"

"Right," I replied. "We're gonna need some waiters."

"Waiters, why wait?" Barry teased. "Let's try them out right now."

Turning back to the boys, I replied, "There can be no tattooing in or around the coffee shop. Let's get to work."

"Manual labor," Gordon said proudly. As if an alarm went off, the other two sprang into action. Gerry ran to Barry's paintbrush and went to work on the woodwork.

Grant grabbed a broom from the corner and started sweeping briskly.

"Wow, you guys snap right to it," I commented.

"We can work for you for an hourly wage then," Gordon told us.

"How much per hour do you want?" I asked.

Gerry tossed the brush back into the paint bucket as if disgusted. Grant dropped the broom on the floor and put his hands on his hips.

I wrote a figure on a scrap of paper and handed it to Gordon. He looked at it, turned it upside down, looked at it from that angle a moment and wrote something on the other side. He handed it back to me.

"They will work for that amount," he motioned to his brothers. "I will work for this."

He set his wage a few dollars more than his brothers. I could use the help to get the place up and running ahead of schedule but his wage was too high.

"No," I said flatly and returned the note to him.

Again he wrote something down and handed it back saying, "Very well, then they will work for this."

When I read it, I smiled. He had left his wage the same and lowered the amount paid to his brothers by one dollar an hour.

"Are you serious?" I asked.

"Still too much?" he asked. "I can lower their wages again if need be." He leaned in close to me and whispered, "They can be trouble. I manage them." He rolled his eyes in the direction of his brothers. "So, we have a deal or not?"

"Sure, we need to get the place ready and open as fast as possible," I replied.

"Okay, men," shouted Gordon. He clapped his hands twice. "Back to work!"

Gerry and Grant flung themselves back into their jobs, rushing to their tools. Gordon walked slowly across the room.

"What about you?" I asked him.

"I'm exhausted. I'll be on break," he answered.

Barry poured him a coffee and they both leaned against the counter sipping away. I gave Barry my best 'I can't believe this' look. He smiled, shrugged and took another sip.

Thinking back to that day we hired the three boys, I knew that the staff would be Barry's main headache while mine would be the food, the finances, the failure, or the glory.

Chapter 3

SUDDENLY, MY REVERIE ABOUT the past weeks was interrupted by an abrupt squeal followed by a hum. The music switched from the Snoop Dog noise the staff had turned on to some of Pat Methaney's mellow intelligent jazz. Barry knew my distain for the trendy *du jour* sound the music industry forced on us. Besides, he didn't want me to be peevish. We needed another batch of freshly prepared salad dressings, a kettle of soup and several other items to satisfy the locals and tourists who were rapidly discovering the tempting, fresh homemade offerings. I did all the prep and cooking; the staff just heated soups and stews and assembled the sandwiches and salads.

"I don't get it. We don't do any advertising; no TV, no

radio, not a single newspaper ad and business is getting better every day. Not just from the locals. But the tourists are showing up like we had a sign outside offering free gasoline with every purchase," Barry commented.

"Two words," I offered.

"Easy sex?"

"No!" I snapped. "Fresh, homemade! That's what's missing in a tourist's vacation. You can't get that under the golden arches or in a grand slam, triple by-pass breakfast. After a few weeks of hotel breakfast buffets and truck-stop ptomaine treasures, you're craving something fresh and original. It's word of mouth advertising."

"You're probably right," he answered. "I notice more and more people coming in because they heard that this is the place to eat. It's not like asking a New Yorker for directions."

"Uh huh, to the gates of Hell…charming."

"Sure, kind of like Parisians with their gracious attitude."

"Try not to be so evasive. I can't quite figure out how you really feel, Mr. Sunshine," I laughed as I returned to my work at the sink.

Just to be annoying, Barry held the ice-cold, caramel coffee out of reach, while I clawed the air, grasping for the tall glass.

"Thanks," I mumbled as my tongue licked the thick drip of caramel syrup running down the side of the glass. "Umm, how'd you make this so good?" I cooed.

"Anything for you, my little Lamb Chop," he laughed.

"Have you changed your mind yet, a little sugar, my Sweet Cinnamon Bun? He raised his eyebrows several times suggestively. After all, we're officially partners." He was trying.

"You're just too young for me, my braised Pig Knuckle," I quipped right back.

"Hey, why let a decade stand in our way," he countered.

"Mmmm, no, I don't think that's a good idea. Let's just see how our deal works out, okay? No complications," I answered, chugging the delicious caramel laced espresso.

"Whatever you say, but you're one sexy mama. I think you put into the food." He was being sweetly persistent. "I've been thinking about us lately."

"*Us*, the magazine? I see it next to *People* and *Entertainment Weekly*, but I'm really not very interested in that trash…"

"No," he interrupted. "I mean us, as in you and me."

"Come on, Barry. I don't want to go into this again."

"Then don't. Let me take you out for coffee."

"We work at a coffee shop, remember," I admonished him while looking around the room. "Well, at least one of us does," I shrugged.

"Okay, bad idea, agreed. How about a late night flick after work? They're showing *Butcher Knives of Blood* at the Movievue on Jordan Road."

"A slasher film? That's what you think I'd like?"

"Hey, it worked for Freddy Kruger," he said apologetically.

I smiled and shook my head in disbelief.

"Wait, I've got it. What about a late night dinner at The Heartline?" Raising an eyebrow, he continued. "Oh yeah, that's it. Fine French wine, a crusty warm baguette, and a double portion of '*Barry le Magnifique*' for the main course. How's that sound?"

"Sounds like I'm on a diet," I answered. Holding a hand to my chest to fain illness, I added, "Now more than ever."

"Oh come on, what's wrong with dating me?" he demanded.

I placed a hand on my hip and tilted my head slightly in that quintessential schoolteacher pose used for centuries to point out the obvious.

"You're right. We don't have that kind of time. Look," he said, producing a slip of paper from his pocket. "I've written a list of things we might enjoy."

I was genuinely touched by the time and thought he'd put into winning my affection. Then, just as quickly, I came to my senses. "A list, that's really nice. I appreciate it. But before I see it, do me a favor."

"Anything for you, my Scrumptious Muffin."

"Okay, first, take off any date that has the prefix nude, naked, see-through, or waterbed." Begrudgingly, he tore the bottom third of the list off and stuffed it back into his pocket.

"Okay, next, remove any idea with the words hot tub, skinny dipping, or strip poker in them." Once again, another third of the paper was torn off and shoved unceremoniously away.

"Finally, remove any date that involves me not getting home on the same night." He rolled the rest of the paper into a ball and tossed it in disgust over his shoulder. I began to laugh and attempted to return to work when he started in again.

"Okay, forget the list. Who do I think I am, Fabio? Besides, I've never been fond of obsession."

"Exactly, I'd peg you for an Old Spice man or maybe Brute."

"Very funny," he said testily. "At these wages, my cologne is 'eau de Sweat ala Brow'."

"Okay already, we've wasted enough time here. Now get these guys out of here and off the clock so I can get this work done. And quick, write me a list of what we've run out of already. I can't remember all the batches you need for tomorrow." I was fried.

"And you write me a list of the toxic stuff in your two soups. The crazies will be back tomorrow."

"Let them go to Denny's!" I blurted out. Shocked at my retort, we both laughed.

Chapter 4

AFTER BARRY MADE ME aware of the requests of the customers, I had to face the problem. This could become an issue that could spell out a new career in coffee shop ownership or financial ruin. My frame of mind was that my creative offerings on the coffee shop menu were more than fine and dandy. The dishes were made with excellent top notch ingredients and care. My first reaction was to ignore Barry's request to list my ingredients partly because my cooking, whether a meal for two, ten, or a gigantic amount for the coffee shop, was done by instinct honed by years of experience and my taste. If I liked it, I served it. And I had a hard time telling others the exact recipe by weight or measure. Volumes, dashes, and estimates, however, abounded in my cooking.

Many measurements were done on the palm of my hand. I could exactly reproduce a restaurant dish that I had tasted in the past over and over again. To pass it along, I would need a scale alongside my hand and an accurate record keeper with pen and paper and a sharp eye. But this was a problem that was bigger than my personal sense of taste. I needed a solution that would satisfy the health issues of my patrons. During this first week of official coffee shop ownership, as our style and direction were taking shape, I was a tad more than belligerent about listing the "offending" ingredients for the eccentric tastes of my crackpot customers. I was already tired from all the months of advance preparations.

But now it was time to tuck in, get cracking, and get the food ready for tomorrow. The coffee shop needed a soup and a stew and since the green chili pork posole took the longest to simmer, I'd start it first. Within minutes, the air was filled with the sweet, rich smell of thick chunks of pork shoulder browning in garlic, onion, and green Hatch chilies. There was a natural wizardry of the chilies' chemistry as it met the heat and it needed to jump into the singular steel-mill cauldron of crackling rage to release the magic in its true flavor. This would be a great batch of green chili posole simmered with slow-cooked vegetables and drowned in spicy gravy. And sometimes I had to remind myself I was working in an eating establishment that had…no kitchen!

After the last pot was put away, the final seasoning stored, the blinds drawn, and the alarm set, I sat alone on the parking lot cement divider outside the coffee shop. I took a few minutes in the silence to be quiet and enjoy the feel of my new enterprise. I sipped a hot Columbian de-café from a paper cup. The stars flickered in the warm mountain air like the dance of lightning bugs I had watched as a child sitting in an apple orchard so long ago. Everything is tenuous: life, business, health, relationships or belongings. All can be removed or lost in less than the time it takes to think of them, a quick star's twinkle. All that's real is immediate and now. In that instant, in just that one unimportant moment, I had everything I could ever want or need. This was my own creation, my Sedona coffee shop and no person or situation could ruin this for me. Coming to terms with what the audience wanted was up to me. I needed a home run out of this business and I worried everyday if I'd strike out.

I watched as the ribbons of steam rose from the cup and softly evaporated in the moonless air of the evening. I thought how lucky I was to be here and smiled to myself. My back throbbed, my muscles ached, my hands and arms felt heavy like iron pipes dangling from my torso. But I was here, alone in a place of mystic and geological beauty unlike anywhere else on Earth. I was convinced God gave me these few moments of contentment to reward me for all the millions of moments others would think unimportant.

From out of the shadows a tall muscular figure approached. It was a Native American man in his forties with long straight, dark hair. He wore a black cowboy hat

33

with a feather, jeans, and a flannel shirt. His movements were like a stealthy bobcat and as he approached a manly waft of hormones met my nose. I felt a chill little wind following him and a gentle shift in the energy field. Without saying a word, he sat next to me and withdrew a pint of Jack Daniels from his pocket.

"May I?" he asked, tilting the bottle in my direction.

I paused for a moment and smiled, "Ah, sure. What the hell." We laughed and toasted our drinks together and looked silently up at the night sky.

"Hey, I'm Bobby. You work here?" he asked.

"Yeah," I answered. "I'm Resa."

I nodded when he passed the bottle to me. As I took a long pull of the sweet liquor I heard Bobby say, "You know something? The lady who owns this place makes a chili just like my Grandma back home on the Third Mesa."

Chapter 5

IT STARTED SOMEWHERE, THIS transition from the field of healthcare to a coffee shop on the corner in an Arizona resort town. Sure, I had been a wife, a mother and had a career that ran the gamut from X-ray technologist to the fund raisers for breast cancer research. Not only had I preformed thousands of mammograms, I had presented breast health lectures at women's groups and seminars. Mine was a familiar face at the ladies' luncheons, award dinners and at the annual *Race for the Cure*.

A mere five months earlier, on a calm, sun-filled Sunday in Phoenix, I innocently canvassed the classified ads. My eyes strayed to the *Businesses for Sale* section. At first, it was fun to read about candy routes, sports bars, pizza joints, sandwich stands, hot-dog trucks, and espresso carts that were for sale. Reading the ads weekend after weekend became a habit and I fantasized about the realities of various occupations. I always wondered if my strength, energy, and hard work could create a business of my own.

It was on one of those rare days, a February morning with a crystalline azure sky overhead, that I lounged on my balcony overlooking a sparkling pool and sipped a hot mocha latte. I was enjoying the best winter weather the country offered when I spotted it, the "ad"; the ad that I just couldn't forget. It kept after me the way a case of poison ivy itches a camping-out Girl Scout. It read:

Sedona Coffee/Sandwich Shop, All equipment, coffee franchise,
Get new lease, established lunchtime clientele $15K
Call Matt 928-204-xxxx

Not only was I intrigued; my mind was working ways and numbers.

Since the ad kept running through my mind, a couple of days later, I consulted my neighbor, Barry Bennett. By that time, I had heard Barry's oral curriculum vitae several times over. He was highly qualified, actually overly qualified. We had gotten into an infrequent but spontaneous practice of sharing a dinner, a bottle of wine and a little laughter. His background included a number of different jobs and a Masters in Psychology. When he grew tired of other people's troubles and complaints and the antics of poor parenting resulting in misled adolescents, he turned to management with big name chains such as Pepsi, Dunkin Donuts, Coffee Plantation, and Cinnabon.

When I asked him to call Matt, the seller, and ask a slate of appropriate business questions, he agreed. He would be the voice to protect me from the prejudice of gender bias that all women face. He would be a shield against my lack of business experience. When I asked him about a quick trip one hundred miles north to look into the opportunity, he replied, "Why not? Any day in Sedona is a great day!"

Those who have never witnessed the greatness and splendor that is Sedona have missed a breath-taking sight. Sedona, Arizona has a backdrop that has framed a multitude of Hollywood motion pictures. It attracts and enchants those individuals on their quest for enlightenment. The presence of the Vortex energy, which amplifies the highs and lows, affects all who live there and visit. So there is a mixture of old glamour and new age consciousness.

First timers have unusual experiences within minutes of arriving and getting a jaw-dropping gawk at the scenery. Thoughts start to stream, promises are made, affirmations start to flow, and accidents begin to abound. If the tourists aren't spellbound by the rock formations, they just don't have a clear view from their car window or from the arrival—four times daily—of the Extra Mile shuttle bus. Many drivers have a fender bender within their first few hours in town. Some say that this is due to the distraction of nature's majesty. Others say that the energy of the

Vortex disrupts those who are not prepared, too heavy with their own dark energy. Tourists come for the scenery or the award winning spas unlike any others on Earth. They want to see the spots where so many old Westerns were filmed, ride to the Back O' Beyond in a Pink Jeep or take a hot air balloon ride. They slip and slide on the loose red rock gravel shattering ankles, wrists, elbows, and knees. Visitors rent horses, ATV's, bikes, and motorcycles that result in cracked skulls and broken ribs. Campers are lured into the gurgling water of Oak Creek whose rocks have algae as slippery as glass. Tibias, forearms, and hips are fractured on a steady basis. Slide Rock has an ice-cold water ride on boulders slicker than oil. Kneecaps, fingers and jawbones crumple against the rush of water, hurdling bodies to the last pool. And if the activities of hiking, sightseeing or touring aren't injurious, then many visitors go wild on the town's restaurant selections and end up with what is called in medical jargon, a "hot belly" due to the excesses of overeating.

In the emergency room at the medical clinic the staff witnesses all this and attends to them all, usually starting about 3:00 PM on any Friday afternoon as the parade of travelers arrive.

Another aspect of Sedona's history is that the early settlers planted a number of apple orchards in the early 1900's; many still exist at the south entrance of Oak Creek Canyon and in the West Fork entrance. An apple grown in Sedona has the sweet perfume and the crispness and crunch lost in the grocery store varieties. The old time heirloom varieties, such as Russet, Winesap, Baldwin, Spitzenberg, and Pippin became a mainstay of the early settlers who counted on the apple crop to get by the winter months. Apples were cooked, dried, canned and cold-stored in all forms and the pioneer women exchanged recipes for anything an apple could produce: cakes, pies, sauces, butters, cider, ciderkins, pectin, vinegar, applejack, calvados, and apple wine.

As a member of the rose family, the pome fruit has a compartmental center of five carpels. Each carpel contains one to three seeds. Cut along the horizontal, a five-pointed star is seen and the spring blossoms each have five petals. Some people believe that the taste of the apple and the fragrance are identical. Many of the old-timers made a skillet apple pie over an outdoor fire. It was a simple breakfast or a hearty dessert consisting of sliced apples, butter and sugar, if available, and a mixture of flour, meal, oats, and leavening. These became known as Apple Betty, Apple Crumble, Apple Crisp, or Pan Dowdy. The City of Sedona pays tribute to the apple with a wooden welcome sign near the Midgley Bridge that depicts an apple tree loaded with red fruit.

There's more to the City of Sedona than breathtaking red rock scenery and apple orchards. It is an area of natural activities: a morning town rather than a nightlife scene. Visitors and town folk arise with the sun in the early morning as light moves on rock face to partake in hiking, hot air balloon rides, fishing, shopping, swimming and biking. For art lovers, it is a base of power. During the day, the opportunity for aura photography, crystal gazing, tarot cards, fortune telling, psychic insights, vortex tours, massage, and spiritual elevation are explored. The valley is a magnet that attracts the wanderers of the Universe. They call Sedona home, arriving to spend some time in a red rock gorge where they refuse to take a course as their compass wiggles, wags, and shakes instead of a true point in any direction.

Chapter 6

THE NEXT TIME BARRY and I had a free day, we headed north for an appointment with the seller of the coffee shop. It was on this scouting mission to Sedona that I first saw the building. Granted, it had something very distinctive in appearance. It was simply stunning! Architecturally designed years ago as a movie theatre on the West side of town, it was striking. Original iron fretwork set it apart from others structures in the area. Windows were eighteen feet tall on this two-story structure. The wrap around patio had at least seventy-five feet of rambling spaces with landscaping that both shaded and buffered the main highway through town. It was situated on the road that led to *The Enchantment*, an internationally known resort. Sizing up the parking lot that could handle over a hundred cars, I estimated that space would never be a problem. Could I do this?

At the present time, there was just one occupant in this huge building, taking up about one-tenth of the total space. As I walked in, I noticed that as impressive and grand the exterior, the sandwich shop was in sharp contrast. It wasn't shabby chic; it was filthy. One wall had every lost soul's card, ad, poster or plea for employment or housing. A crooked sign above the counter gave a limited selection of sandwich choices. The refrigerated display case was a hodgepodge of stored groceries used to build the sandwiches. On top of the case, a bevy of freshly basked pastries and muffins were laid open to the air, dust and flying insects.

In spite of an agreed upon appointment time, no one named Matt materialized. After a few minutes of waiting, Barry suggested we use the time as a spy mission. One of his many past positions had been as a detective. He began counting customers, estimating the average bill while I was sizing up the efficiency of the two girls behind the counter and the potential of a coffee shop makeover. One young girl had a sleeping infant behind the counter in a playpen. A baby stroller was parked in a corner. The natural stonewall at the entrance was a chunk of the outdoors brought inside. Features such as the space and the roominess were major pluses. There were twelve tables that could seat four and the vaulted ceiling height made my thoughts about the potential as high as the stratosphere. We were munching on fresh sandwiches and strong coffees wondering about Matt's appearance when my cell phone rang.

"Come on down to the village, to the Cactus Flower Bakery. I can't break away," Matt instructed.

As we wound our way down Highway 89A to the "Y" and hooked up with Route 179, the fog was starting to lift. Along with the natural wonder of Sedona's beauty is the fact that the look is constantly shifting. The four seasons, the clouds, shadows, sunshine, and the passage of the sun on rock walls all create an ever-changing pallet. Today, Mother Nature's spectacle was the contrast of snow streaks on red rock.

We found Matt Richards's main business about twenty minutes later in the Village of Oak Creek, commonly called the V.O.C. As we entered the bakery, the stereo blared outdated sixties hits. The place had a great smell of baked goods. Barry took in the room like an accountant at a casino.

"The table space and seating capacity isn't being used properly. If you rearrange a few things and add some counter seating or window seats, you could easily double the seating capacity," he instructed.

"Barry, I'm impressed."

"Well shucks, Ma'am," he said in a cowboy drawl. "Ya'll know I'm not just another pretty face here at the bunkhouse. Why, I gots me some real book learnin' an everything. Why, I'd count to twenty-one fer ya, but I'd have to take my pants off."

I gave him a swift elbow to the ribs and he stopped.

He enjoyed embarrassing me as often as possible, but it was becoming tougher for him as I became familiar with his antics.

He pointed to the cashier. "Check out the two girls behind the counter. They've spent more time flirting than working. They're falling all over one another to wait on a handsome man while that elderly woman and her friends might as well have coated themselves with deadly plutonium for all the attention they're getting."

I examined the room to see a large dog sleeping in one of the corners. I motioned to Barry to get his reaction.

"I'm not sure what the health department regulations are, but I'm fairly confident a canine doesn't qualify as a garbage disposal no matter how well it works," he told me.

"I don't mean to be petty but I haven't seen those girls clean up once in the time we've been here," I said.

"Are you kidding? I keep wondering who cleans up after them," Barry laughed.

Within minutes, I was beginning to realize that extreme casualness was the order of the day in and around Matt's businesses. Matt spotted us and hurried around the counter, shaking flour off his hands to extend a greeting.

"You found the bakery, okay. Let's sit over here and talk business, if you guys got some dough, ha, ha, ha," Matt chuckled.

He was a twitchy-nosed wiggler who had the unnerving habit of raising his upper lip, revealing large Chicklet-shaped teeth, as he spoke. I tried not to stare at the mustache that looked like whiskers on a ferret.

"Okay, so you saw the coffee shop. Was Nina there?" he asked.

"Uh huh, she and another girl," I replied.

Matt was dressed like a used car salesman and he talked like a late night television pitchman. If you didn't know better, you'd swear he was the guy you saw at the State Fair selling kitchen-chopping devices from an outdoor booth. He leaned forward in his chair and cleared his throat. It was as if he were about to reveal some private information or divulge a national security secret.

"I leased the space as a second location for product overflow. But more important, it gave my warden, the little missus, a place to keep busy, to feel like she was doing something, you know, to keep her outta my way."

Barry and I were taken aback by Matt's quick familiarity. We both looked at each other in astonishment. Matt noticed and tried in his own delicate way to explain.

"Hey," he smiled. "Don't get me wrong. She was a fairly good wife for a while. She'd laugh at my jokes, made a fairly decent martini and never nagged.

This was becoming laughable. For the sake of business, I bit my tongue and said, "I know how you feel. Next thing you know, women will want to vote." The sarcasm was either over his head or through the hole in it.

He laughed nervously and continued, "Anyhow, that was five years ago."

"Ah ha," Barry and I were all ears.

"Then about two years ago, things start gettin' a little

hinky-dinky with her."

On the long list of things I didn't need to know, Matt's love life had to be at the very top. I tried to change the subject. "Well, you know, we really don't need to know…"

"No, no, I want to tell ya," he laughed. "You'll get a kick out of this. Like I was saying, things start to go sideways between us. She hires a pool boy with a day job. The guy can only stop by at night. This seems kinda weird since I never see any tools or truck or anything. But I'm working late most of the time, or out with the guys, so I blow it off."

"Shouldn't we get back to business? We're on a schedule and…," Barry said.

"Yeah, yeah, I'm getting to the good part," Matt explained.

"To think it gets better than this," I mumbled under my breath.

Oblivious to my remarks, Matt continued, "So out of nowhere she fires the pool boy and starts taking guitar lessons from some folk singer in Oak Creek Canyon. Only she has to go to his place for the lessons. I offered to buy her a guitar but she says she's been playin' with his instrument."

"That's awful," Barry consoled.

"You're telling me. That bum was a lousy teacher. She took lessons sometime five nights a week. She never missed a single lesson. Then six months later we're at a friend's house who owns a guitar. She couldn't play a note. That creep was ripping us off. And here I was paying a hundred bucks a week. Can you believe that?"

"I'm having a hard time with it," smirked Barry.

"Apparently so was she," I added with a smile.

Matt wrinkled his face, shrugged and continued undaunted, "So, like I was saying, things started to raise my suspicion a little after that. She took up yoga, massage therapy, riding lessons. That started to make me think."

"I'm shocked," I whispered.

"Oh, I was shocked too," Matt went on. "I'm pretty sure she had something going on with that guy. I mean he was nice enough and all. Sometimes he'd pick her up for her lessons right here at the house. But I put an end to things when her car broke down and she had to stay overnight after a yoga lesson."

Trying to defuse the embarrassing conversation, I offered, "Well, if she was stranded there's not much she could do."

"The guy lived down the block," Matt remarked.

Barry and I looked at each other and grimaced in response. Then Barry thought momentarily and asked, "Well if he lived so close, I don't understand why you just didn't walk over and…"

"The game was on," Matt answered in a matter of fact manner. Barry nodded and looked at me explaining, "It's a guy thing."

Those two were engaged in a testosterone carnival and I wanted to get to the business at hand. I countered, "Well, let's get back to the deal about the coffee shop."

"Hey, I'm all business. You know what people say

about me?" Matt asked rhetorically.

"Yes, but I'd rather not repeat it in mixed company," Barry quipped.

"Exactly, they say Matt Richards is all business. That's what they say," he bragged. "Anyway, now she's the Ex, you know what I mean?"

"Ah ha," we answered in unison.

"So I put my best worker, Nina, down there, a great gal I met from Florida. You know, to run the place while the divorce was going on."

"Ah ha."

"Nina is just a half pint, five foot nothing but a hard worker. Then she gets married and pregnant. Boom, like that! Still runs the West End shop all through her pregnancy. Don't know how she did it, but I found out she couldn't keep up. Started opening up late, sometimes not at all. Closing up early. I was losing money and customers. I hired her some help but they come and go, ya know?"

"Mmmmm!" I nodded, listening intently.

"Then the old lady wants her share of the money outta the business; still have to settle, so I need to sell. And I want to bring Nina back here to the village cause she knows all my recipes. Customers love her big smile and they love the baby. So, what are you two looking for?" Matt asked abruptly. He swung his gaze back and forth between Barry and me looking for a hint.

While I pulled back in my chair a little and tried to come up with a non-committal answer, Barry leaned forward, now on the offensive. He gave his throat a quick warm-up. This was his forte. I let him do the talking.

"Well, Resa and I might be looking to relocate and pick up a business. After all, she's a great cook and I have experience in management with. . ." and he started ticking off his former stints with the corporations, the transfers, the job responsibilities.

Since I heard it all before and knew this could take a while, I decided to take some visual notes of the bakery. Behind the counter everything was coated with a thick layer of flour. The cases were erratically filled with some scrumptious looking goodies; fruity Danish, croissants, brioche, and cream puffs stuffed with lemon custard. Right then and there I decided to snag a luscious looking chocolate volcano cake. It was priced at $4.50 a single serving, but it promised to give me an indication of Matt's wares. Above the counter were stacks of freshly baked breads of all flavors and types: French style batards, baguettes, some ryes, and sourdoughs.

The décor was a mixed media of amateurish sponge painting on the walls. To make up for the lack of décor, the air was perfumed with the yeasty smell of freshly baked bread. The ovens gave off warmth against the outside chilled, winter air.

I turned toward the guys and cleared my throat, "Say, Matt?" I had nibbled on the edge of the luscious chocolate cake. "Which chocolate do you use for these? I can't tell if it's a Guittard or a Scharflen Berger?"

"Wrong," was all he answered. His glasses slid down

his nose and he stared at me.

"Ghirardelli, Valrhona, maybe an El Rey?" I asked.

"WRONG, WRONG, WRONG!"

"Can I have the recipe? I asked.

"Not in a million years," he stated flatly. "That little cake is my gold mine and costs me as much to make." He went back to the business at hand with Barry.

"It's easy. You apply to the landlord for a new lease. Here's his name. Buy what you see – lock, stock, and bagel, ha, ha, ha!"

Matt wasn't funny. People were calling him from behind the counter, asking him questions. He looked nervous and fidgety. We had been there less than a half-hour. I interjected we might have more questions after we discussed this first meeting.

Matt answered with a, "Got to get back to work," and "First come, first served," and "Ha, ha, ha, first money down takes it."

As we strolled out into the sunshine peaking through the clouds, I had a real strong wish to go sit in the Chapel of the Holy Cross and light a candle because I knew prayers made there were answered. As we climbed inside the car, shouting our goodbyes and "We'll be in touch," I heard Matt's voice call out.

"Oh, hey, one more thing," he was calling from the front door, his head peaking out a crack.

"Yeah?" I questioned, a stupid smile on my face.

"When you were over there, you saw that there's no kitchen, right?" The fact was delivered as his rodent-like whiskers of a mustache disappeared into the bakery. He was gone, sucked back into his floury empire.

The mile-high mountain air was cold, sweet, and fresh; it was laced with the vanilla and yeasty vapors floating from the door. The small sack I cradled was still warm from the oven and the chocolate volcano cake was oozing a buttery goodness onto my hands. Hooking up the seatbelt, I relaxed, my eyes going into a blank glaze. My mind was working hard, snapshots doing a mental search of the run-down sandwich shop that I had seen just an hour earlier. We had seen industrial equipment, under counter refrigerators, two display cases, yards and yards of stainless steel. No kitchen?

Barry and I were silent for a few minutes, both wondering about the curve ball that Matt had just thrown. As we drove away, the slalom like curves threw us from side to side. We stared ahead, our minds puzzled. No real kitchen?

"What was it that we saw?" The question filled the car and blanked out the gorgeous scenery whizzing by the windows. Barry raised his shoulders in a defeated shrug, sped up and steered the car straight back to the sandwich shop.

We raced past the Outdoor Sports Center and narrowly missed a couple of wobbly bike riders trying to get into traffic. Barry slowed down and swerved to miss them, his mind sorting out the meeting with Matt. We counted off on our fingers what we remembered about the equipment.

"What did you see?" I asked.

Barry said, "There was a chilled make table."

"What's that?" I asked.

"The make table is the assembly line. It holds all the ingredients in big pans for sandwiches and salads. It's a cooler below. That's where you get your orders made," Barry informed me.

"Okay," I said, my mind worked around maximizing the productivity and efficiency of the space to its full potential. There were eight to ten feet of stainless steel prep counters. A commercial Viking oven was set too low for easy access but was a roomy oven nevertheless. There were two heavy-duty *La Pavoni* espresso machines and three wash basins. Facing the dining room were two large Taylor refrigerated display cases and a huge iced tea-brewing station. I saw the Kitchen Aid commercial dishwasher and smelled the rank garbage in the sink room.

"Barry, what did Matt mean, 'No kitchen?'" I felt bewildered and lost outside of my area of expertise.

We screeched into the empty parking lot and ran up to the locked front doors. The acacia trees were budding and daffodil sprouts peeked green tips skyward. The sandwich shop was closed yet the sign clearly stated hours till 5:00 PM on Saturdays. Barry was on the street side of Highway 89 A, shading me from the low slant of the winter sun. He cupped his chubby hands around his eyes to improve his peripheral vision. He shifted his heft from foot to foot and the steam-engine cadence of his mouth-breathing huffed his excitement.

"Ah, ah, I see a shitty wall color and filthy turf carpeting.

Hand me a blowtorch."

"It needs a makeover," I said.

"Have you got the bank for that, Sugarplum?"

"Stop with the terms of endearment, Barry. You're here to check out the business, not me."

"Whatever," he replied.

We peeked into the dust-streaked windows. What could 'no kitchen' really mean amid the many feet of shiny stainless steel?

"Can you see anything?" I asked, smearing a spit-moistened circle on the glass to make a peephole.

"Look's like a kitchen to me," Barry replied.

"Barry, I want my business card to be over a thin slab of good dark chocolate."

"What?"

"I can't decide. Will I name it the Coffee Shop on the Corner, Coffee on the Rocks or maybe the Weathervane Café….?"

"Already naming a place you just saw two hours ago for the first time?" He had a defiant tone in his voice. "You're making decisions before I can tell you what I think. Isn't that why I'm here?"

"That's why you're here." I was multiplying the table sides by the number of chairs and placing white cloths and bud vases on the tabletops.

"You think we can do this, Barry?" I asked.

"Beat's me, Love Dumpling."

Just then a chilly wind swooshed under my skirt and blew red rock dust up my nose. A jolt of frighteningly cold lightening shot through my lower spine; the stab came from a finger attached to a strange creature. Behind me, an unfamiliar reedy voice whispered.

"Maybe whoever owns the shop plans to remove the kitchen and sell the parts to make some extra cash," came a wraspy female voice.

We turned to see a woman of indeterminate age wearing a multi-colored robe and scarf over her head like the women of Slavic countries. Her neck was adorned with beads and charms. She looked like she stepped right out of Central Casting for a Bella Lugosi horror movie. She was half-hag, half-gypsy.

"Is there going to be a full moon tonight?" Barry asked.

She looked straight ahead without turning to acknowledge us as she continued, "You can't blame anyone for getting all they can out of this. They want to get back whatever they can before the curse gets them."

"The curse?" I asked.

"I've said too much already. I should leave," she said, and turned to walk away.

"No wait," I said.

"Resa, you heard the lady. She's got to go. Besides, her broom is probably double parked."

"No, I want to hear this," I told him.

Barry whispered, "That's fine, maybe she can e-mail you from the sanitarium when she gets home later."

I gave him a scowl and turned back to the mysterious guest. "What about the curse?"

"This land is stained with an evil energy. The building

upon it is cursed for eternity." She stopped abruptly, then added, "I've said too much."

Barry patted her shoulder gently and started to push her away. He smiled anxiously and said, "Maybe you have." Turning to me, wide-eyed, he mouthed, "Coo coo, kook coo."

"Cut it out," I said, my attention back to her. I clasped her boney hands gently in mine and asked, "Please tell me about the curse. I need to know."

The fact was I didn't need to know. I just thought it interesting to learn the local lore and folk stories. She really wanted to tell us; otherwise, she wouldn't have started the conversation in the first place.

"In the days of the wild wolf and open sky," she began.

"De det det de, de det det de," Barry began humming the opening music from the *Twilight Zone*.

I gave him a look that shut him up and she continued, "Long ago, before the white man and the wheel, before the plunder and the plow, this was sacred Native American land. And upon this spot lay an ancient site for healing to be used only by the High Shaman of the tribe."

Her hands shook as she spoke and her eyes seemed to look right through us, as if she were seeing something we couldn't. Her stick-like index finger trembled as she pointed into the distance.

"That is why this place and any structure built upon it is cursed forever. You must believe me," she pleaded.

"Oh, I believe we're cursed. Why else would someone be trying to talk us to death," quipped Barry.

I was having fun now and wanted to know a bit more. "There must be some way to break the curse or cleanse the area?" I asked.

"Sure there is. And I bet it involves paying Madame Mayhem here a large sum of money," said Barry.

"Your money can't help you," she spat. "The curse can only be broken by atonement to appease the spirit gods. Blood or love."

"Blood!" he yelled, as he did a double take. "Okay, now you've gone too far. I can't stand the sight of blood, especially my own. I have to wear a blindfold just to drink a Bloody Mary. Resa, you tell her, once I spilled ketchup on my shirt and fainted."

"Relax, relax, let her explain," I told him.

"The curse must be lifted to make peace with the spirit of the Shaman. Life for a life, blood sacrificed for blood taken," she said in an almost threatening tone. We both stood motionless as she repeated, "Life for life, blood for blood."

"Just our luck she took drama lessons from Hannibal Lecter," said Barry.

I smiled and asked, "Have you ever thought that a life used for good might make amends to the spirits?"

"Come on," whispered Barry. "Let her go before they close her crypt for the night, will ya?"

I'm not a student of the occult or one of those persons fascinated by stories of Bigfoot or the Loch Ness Monster but I was intrigued by this woman's firm belief and tenacity in reaffirming this legend. I wanted to see if she could be swayed.

"I was told a curse can't be passed to a new generation," I informed her.

"Is that true?" asked Barry.

"I doubt it. I just made it up," I whispered.

The woman began slowly backing away, her finger still pointing in our direction. "Life for life, blood for blood," she repeated in a slow almost moaning fashion.

"If that doesn't make your skin crawl, it's on too tight," said Barry as we watched her leave while the chant, "Life for life, blood for blood" still echoed as she disappeared.

"She's harmless, can't you see that?"

"As harmless as a case of E-coli from a week old cheese blintz."

"Don't be silly. She's daffy, not dangerous. The sweet old girl likes to scare the tourists. I'll bet she's a grandmother and volunteers at the hospital."

"Sure, at the blood bank."

"Couldn't you see how much she enjoyed being mysterious? That whole legend of the shaman, oooh scary." I waved my fingers in Barry's face, mocking him. I wiped a smudge of red rock dirt off Barry's nose. "She loved telling it and she loved the fact that it scared you."

"Well, I'm glad I could brighten Morticia's day."

"She's the kind of person that gives this place personality," I explained.

"She's the kind of person that gives this place the creeps."

Chapter 7

I<small>T WASN'T A QUICK</small> decision. Actually, the deliberations of buying the coffee shop took many hours of what-ifs, debating the pros and cons and the huge downside of becoming business owners. And there were many hurtles. Namely, the first and most confounding of all was the finances. Barry's input would be management skills and sweat equity. To give him his due credit, he tried to talk me out of the idea.

Hovered over the kitchen table back at my Phoenix home, Barry and I went over the probable pitfalls and potential problems of the business. A myriad of papers and notes cluttered the area between us as we poured over every scenario we could imagine.

Maybe I was just a bit too confident that my hard work

was the winning ticket. Counting on the large quantities of delicious food that I knew I could turn out, the place would become a hit. I presented Barry with one inspired picture after picture: a photo-montage of optimism.

Barry was objective and analytical to the smallest detail. His business acumen was impressive as he kept a constant eye on the bottom line. He juggled expenses versus possible intake to perceive any situation that might arise. Rising from his chair, he made several chicken scratches on his yellow legal pad and slapped it back onto the table.

"I'm sorry but it's just too risky. With all the overhead and the improvements needed, you might not see any real profit for a full year," he warned.

"Nothing?"

"No, of course you'll generate money, a flow, but I wouldn't put the down payment on the Lamborghini right away. With labor costs you might be paying yourself a really meager salary just to get by at first."

Barry wasn't actually talking to me. He was thinking out loud with me as the audience. I'd learned from past experience to go along with whatever he said until he came to a final conclusion. He stalked up and down the room.

"You're right," I agreed. "I'll invest in something more stable."

"But on the other hand, with your knowledge of food and the expendable income in the Sedona area, it seems like a jackpot ready to pay off."

"That's what I originally thought."

Barry now began to pace back and forth. "But you've got to be cautious. Eighty percent of restaurants fail in the first two years. It's like playing Russian roulette with your bank account. I'd sooner invest in a tanning booth in the Bahamas."

"I don't know what I was thinking. Let's call it off."

"No, there's no reason to panic. If we can keep expenses down by finding reasonable suppliers, you could be seeing a profit much sooner than my first estimate."

"Great, I knew we could work it out."

"Hold on to your wallet, Ms. Greenspan. There are a lot of economic variables here. You don't want to spend your golden years wearing a red vest and welcoming people to K-Mart, do you?"

"Of course not, you're absolutely right. It's entirely too risky," I agreed.

"I didn't say that. I mean, after all, I'd hate to see the ATM spit out hundred dollar bills while you're trying to make a living on the five-cent slots. I don't want you to miss a great opportunity."

"I'd still have my income from my medical job. It's not as if I'm giving up my career."

"Exactly, and if I can find something part-time for you, after eight hours at your day job and ten hours at the coffee shop, you can deliver a few pizzas between hospital shifts, sleep deprivation, and extreme exhaustion," he pointed out.

"Sounds great, I'll check with my therapist. If he likes the idea, I'll sign up for more therapy."

Suddenly Barry stopped pacing, as if completely shocked. "Hey! I'll tell the bad jokes around here if you don't mind, Puddin' Head."

There was a short moment of silence. I started to smile and Barry followed. Before we knew it, we were both laughing at our completely ridiculous conversation.

When our laughter stopped, Barry sat down across from me. His face turned serious as he spoke. "It is risky. But it's a good location and with your taste and talent for design and food, I don't have any doubt you can create a great business. Will the money hold out and patrons grow fast enough to make it successful? That's the one question I can't answer, and unfortunately the most important one of all."

"So?"

"So, if it was my money and I had your talent, I'd do it, but it's not, and I don't, so I'm advising you not to. Did that make any sense at all?"

"Not really," I said. "But I understand what you're trying to say and appreciate your concern."

"So you're taking my advice and forgetting all this?"

"No, I'm going to go for it," I told him. My face showed a confidence and calm but inside I was quivering like a saucer of tomato aspic on the arm of a drunken waiter.

"I knew you would," he laughed.

♦♦♦♦♦♦♦♦♦♦♦

We took a second spy mission up north to do our

research, asking questions of the locals and getting the background scoop. First hand experience, as always, is the only teacher. There was nothing really to sway that decision to move ahead; nothing really insurmountable to block the decision to move forward. There was just a very long list of tasks to make it all work. Move a residence, rent out my Phoenix property, find a suitable home in Sedona, negotiate a contract with the landlord, raise the cash, gain credit, learn the ins and outs of running a business, develop a vision, and follow through on every detail. Against better advice, I slowly moved toward that end always thinking…can I do it, can I do it?

I wasn't hoping for anything other than a business relationship with Barry. He was too young and had a background very different from mine. It was his business management skills and chutzpah that I needed. I could pull together the cash and rodeo the details for the pleasure of residing in Sedona, a little slice of heaven. What I wanted was to live there; no smog, no traffic, no commute, and the chance to be my own boss.

Red Rock Fever, so named by the locals, was never my malady. That's the illness that is akin to a sickness called Blue Sky. Here in the Southwest, people come in droves to follow the economy which has been growing in leaps and bounds decade after decade. The term means that once a new resident experiences a mild winter and gets a long gander at the long expanse of cerulean horizon, a distorted reality of the ease of Arizona life transpires.

Since Sedona is only one hundred miles away by car, a

lovely drive less than two hours north of Phoenix, I could access Sedona anytime I wanted. My fantasy followed the saying, "Do what you love; the money will follow." It probably came straight out of California thinking. It was my blind optimism and the desire to throw the dice for the first time in my life; I was willing to place a bet on myself. I had a touch of the gambler in my soul. It never was Red Rock Fever.

Chapter 8

THERE WAS A SNOWSTORM of blizzard proportions when the start-up paperwork began. During March, I was still strongly wavering about the huge portent of actual business ownership. I knew enough from partnering years ago with my sister and her Scottsdale retail store, Small Fortunes, that the recordkeeping alone was a mountain of work. Libras are not known for details of their past expenditures, instead mostly for being excellent shoppers and spenders. My dive into the initial applications was still in the research and development phase; I could pull back at any moment. If I looked at it as a gamble, I was willing to bet $50K on myself, an investment in me. The bank told me, based on my credit history alone, a $40K business loan was in my pocket.

To cover all the financing possibilities, I decided to submit the necessary paperwork to the downtown Small Business Administration and follow up with an appointment.

Walking into the administration's outer office, I felt nervous but confident. It was that mixture of early morning energy and caffeine that propelled me. According to all the information on their website, I had all the qualifications they sought for a startup business. According to their prerequisites, I was a good investment.

The office was dimly lit with dull, cream-colored walls and worn, darkened woodwork. With my Coach bag under one arm and a folder full of documents and papers under the other, I stood at the receptionist's window in the center of the room waiting for acknowledgement. The secretary before me sat at her desk and continued her work, not bothering to look up at me. She was a middle-aged woman with mousey brown hair that she wore in a bun so tight I thought her eyes might pop out at any moment. It helped pull her forehead up in a mock face-lift.

Behind her to the right, an open door allowed me to see the administrator sitting at his desk. He wasn't working; he didn't appear to be doing anything. He looked right at me making full eye contact but made no attempt to react.

I stood there clumsily and watched the second hand circle the clock dial behind the secretary's desk four times. Finally, I cleared my throat hoping to get her attention.

"I see you," she said without looking up from her

work.

"My name is…"

"I know what your name is. You're here for your 9:00 AM appointment," she said.

"Yes, Mr. Sullivan is expecting me…"

"Mr. Sullivan is busy now. He'll be with you in a moment," she said in a strict tone.

Looking past her, I saw Mr. Sullivan sitting at his desk, still doing nothing whatsoever. Just the same, I was here with hat-in-hand, so I smiled awkwardly and looked around for a place to sit.

Without looking up the secretary announced, "You can take a seat out in the hall. There's a bench there."

Stepping into the hallway, I saw the bench she was apparently referring to. It was at least thirty feet away, near the stairwell. I turned back to ask, "Pardon me, is it going to be a while, maybe I should…"

"You should wait in the hallway like I just told you," she said sternly.

At nine forty-two, I was still sitting in the hallway waiting for my appointment. I started to worry they'd forgotten about me so I walked back into the office.

"Miss, I'm sorry to bother you but I've been waiting for quite a while now and I was just…"

"I know how long you've been waiting," she interrupted.

I cut her off saying, "Then you know I've been waiting almost an hour."

"I know how to tell time!"

"Is there a problem? I was told the nine o'clock is the first appointment of the day" I asked.

"What do you expect me to do?"

"Your job, nothing more, nothing less," I told her.

"I don't have to take this," she said indignantly.

"You're right, I'll handle this myself." I walked passed her and directly into Sullivan's office. He didn't have a single paper on his desk, wasn't on the phone and no one was in the office with him.

I sat down and announced in a calm, self-assured voice, "I'm here for my 9:00AM appointment, Mr. Sullivan. That is…. I slowly looked across the top of his empty desk to make my point.

The secretary had stormed in after me. Before she could speak, he raised his hand and told her, "It's alright, luckily I just freed up my calendar." He waved her away.

"So what's your problem?" he asked.

I was thinking, 'My problem is that I'm forced to deal with a couple of do-nothing rejects that shouldn't be given the keys to the soda machine, let alone the finances of entire business operations but what I answered was, "My problem?"

"Well, I mean, why are you here? What do you need?"

"I sent you my business proposal several weeks ago. I brought a copy with me but I presume you're already familiar with it."

He was caught off guard. I could tell he hadn't bothered to read my proposal or even my loan application and had no idea what I was asking to finance. I smiled politely and withdrew my copy of the application from my folder. I slid it across the desk for his examination. He opened it and fanned through it like a blackjack dealer playing cards from the bottom of the deck.

"You realize we can't just hand out money willy-nilly to everyone with their hands out?" he said in a demeaning way.

"I understand that. I have an excellent credit history and have a business plan that shows an expected profit margin that will ensure repayment of the loan within a two year period," I explained.

He smiled and dropped the application on the desk as if to completely dismiss me.

"Now that's all well and good but there are certain aspects of your proposal I'm frankly quite worried about."

"Name one," I said, calling his bluff.

"Well, ah, I can't say exactly. I can't name them off the top of my head. But there are several items that a more savvy businessman would be wary of."

I was burning up. He had absolutely no intention of even considering my application. And the sexist remark about 'a more savvy businessman' versus 'business person' was frosting me.

"It's a sound proposal. If you'll just take the time to go over the statistics with me, I think you'll see it's based on sound research," I offered.

"Oh, I'm sure it has its good parts," he consoled.

I resented his pandering and since he'd already decided against me, I no longer had to overlook his attitude. "So just for my own information, what did you think of my idea to increase revenue by valet parking on weekend nights," I asked.

"Well," he said, sitting back in his chair and laughing. When I first saw it in your proposal, I thought it was industrious but maybe just a little over zealous. If you know what I mean."

"There is no valet parking idea in my proposal. I just made that up. You never read it, did you?"

"Well, ah, I guess I'm getting it confused with another report. I get a lot of them you know. Why don't we set up another appointment six weeks from now after you revise your business plan and include a professionally prepared five-page proforma."

"My performa is included in the document you have and I need my answer within three weeks."

Mr. Sullivan looked at me with snake eyes and I knew then that the game was over and the dice roll had crapped out.

"That's simply impossible, Ms. Milan. I suggest you consider other alternatives." The meeting was over.

After the unsavory visit to the Small Business Administration, I decided to go private and budget every nickel. On a daily-to-weekly basis during that sunny March, I encountered a progressive series of steps toward the apex of buying a business in the real world. Maybe I could pull this off by myself with Barry out front. Before any other plans were made, a trip to the landlord's office in Flagstaff would be the next challenge.

Chapter 9

NO ONE WILL EVER tell you about the wind in Sedona. You'll hear about so many other things... like the rock formations, the canyon, the creek, the wildlife, the ruins, and the petro glyphs, but not the wind. There is never any warning about how it comes out of nowhere. It juts around from any direction any time of day, any season, no rhyme, no reason and no prediction. Maybe it's all the diverse rock formations that send the drafts in serpentine currents. The local Hindustani call it "Vayu." Whatever it is, there is no foretelling its arrival. Long ago, Shakespeare penned a line about a scolding wind. Here the wind was a mischievous imp playing rude and annoying tricks on us.

In the Provence region of France, the farmers are

besieged by the mistrals, which can drive sane minds to distraction. In the fall, Californians dread the havoc and wildfire spreading destruction of the Santa Ana winds.

In Sedona you can never trust that one element. The perfidious wind will come out of nowhere on a perfectly calm and sunny day and reek damage and destruction. Even the Native Americans have a name for every direction that the blowing wind takes. Today it is "Shawondasee," or the South Wind, blowing first in one direction then abruptly changing course like a wild mustang racing maddeningly to and fro along a fence seeking an escape.

In March, stormy weather and sudden winds are expected as spring arrives in the high country of Arizona. In spite of balmy breezes and golf course weather in Phoenix, I packed winter gear into the back bay of my palomino-colored SUV, fondly nicknamed, Work Horse, a trusty steed of pistons, fossil fuel, and two-hundred-eighty-five horsepower and headed north to Flagstaff and to the snow. The sole of my hand-tooled Lamas pushed the throttle. As Highway 17 climbs in elevation, stands of saguaros cactus running for miles mark a change between the microcosms of the Sonoran Desert and the adjacent growth of junipers in the highlands. My reliable old girl, Work Horse, pulled at a steady speed up the treacherous curves past Bumble Bee and Crown King. She easily mounted the last crest at Sunset Point without so much as a shudder or a heave. I brought along my "bedlam terror", as I referred to my faithful canine, a Bedlington Terrier, named, Skye, who brought up the rear. Barry was riding the shotgun position. As we rode, he talked incessantly about subjects as varied as how long it took for a banana to turn brown in his refrigerator to how many miles per gallon he clocked on his last tank of gas. He finished a long description of which parking spot he last took when getting home from work.

The Mogollon Rim slanted in a spine of elevations upwards to my right about thirty miles in the distance. The silhouettes of the mountain peaks and mesas gradually faded into lighter shades of ochre and grays as they retreated from sight. In another hundred miles, my truck would have us at our destination in time for the appointment with the landlord, Bernard Stein.

The town of Flagstaff curls around the base of Mount Humphreys. We were headed there for an appointment at the commercial realty company. They housed their office in a building exuding charm and an antique romance of another time. The era was vintage 1890's. A steep black walnut staircase creaked comfort and exclusivity on every tread. The climb to the second floor was a gasping, lung-rattling, breathless pull twenty feet uphill at a sixty-degree slant. The old wood smelled like luxury and money.

Barry accompanied me for the meeting with Mr. Stein. First, we'd be dealing with his assistant, Ms. Esperanza. As we entered the office, we were greeted by a young woman in her mid-twenties with a mane of blonde hair tangled into haphazard patterns resembling last week's French braids. She wore a long denim skirt and a white muslin blouse. Although she wore no visible make-up, she accented her outfit with a half-dozen large bracelets and three beaded, turquoise necklaces. She was far too young to be a part of the 60's generation but the look was a throwback to the counter-culture lifestyle.

She was sipping an energy drink from a can with one of those bent hospital straws when we entered. She looked up and jumped.

"Oh my gosh, you guys startled me," she said in rich kid, up-speak. She put her free hand on her heart. Holding her can out, she continued, "You called earlier, you must be Resa and Barry or is it Barry and Resa?"

"That depends on which one of us you happen to see first, doesn't it?" Barry asked.

She responded with a quizzical expression then turned the limp attention she had to me. "And you must be...?"

I was stunned by her lack of concentration. I looked over at Barry to see a broad grin staring back at me.

"I'm Resa," I told her.

She slapped her forehead with her palm saying, "Duh, I've been so busy today I can't seem to keep anything straight."

"Oh, my gosh, you are so right," said Barry in a valley girl accent. He was off on one of his comedy tangents again. I should've stopped him but he had already perched himself on the corner of her desk. Pointing to her drink, he said, "I love this stuff. Makes my head all... bubbly, I think."

"You too?" she squealed. "Sometimes, when I drink my soda too fast or if I bend over right after taking a big gulp, the bubbles go right up my nose."

"Me too," Barry cooed, "But sometimes I like that." They both giggled aimlessly. Barry gave me a quick wink and helped himself to a handful of cheesy popcorn from an open bag on her desk.

"Miss…" I began to say.

She interrupted, saying, "Oh, I'm Moonbeam, changed it from Evelyn. "

"Pardon me?"

"Moonbeam. That's my name. But my friends call me other things," she explained.

"I can imagine," said Barry, raising his eyebrows.

She gave him a look of conspiracy and they both giggled in response.

"Can you tell Ms. Esperanza we're here?" I asked.

"Sure," she replied, but did nothing.

"Could you do it now, please?" I asked in a hushed, overly polite tone.

"Why not?" she declared with a smile and disappeared behind a heavy wooden door.

"I'm going to stay out here with brain-dead Barbie," Barry announced.

"Why?"

"It'll make you look more independent. Besides, I can keep anyone else that shows up here busy so you'll get as much time as you need in there," he insisted. Before I could object, Moonbeam returned.

"You can go right in," she announced, opening the door.

74

Barry mouthed, "I'll stay here" to Moonbeam, who squeaked and clapped her hands together.

I entered an office decorated in dark wood, brass lamps and wood-slat blinds. It was a great backdrop for a Mickey Spillane novel. While Moonbeam, the receptionist, gave off an air of reckless indifference, Ms. Esperanza was Stein's bad cop assistant. She was a svelte Latina armed with a community college degree. She burned with a loyalty to her boss and interviewed his clients with a hostile combativeness. Her short, straight, ebony hair and high cheekbones gave her the stylish look of a woman on the rise. Following every order Stein gave her, she wore her two-piece business suit like a military uniform.

"Come in, sit down please," she said with the tone of a general.

I sat down and pulled my chair closer to her huge desk.

She was going over the paperwork I'd faxed her. "So you want to lease one of our business properties, is that it?"

"Yes, that's it," I answered in a robotic monotone equal to hers.

"I noticed your partner didn't bother to come in."

"Your boss didn't either," I replied.

"I can work independently of him."

"So can I."

"We're not convinced you can be successful," she bluntly stated.

"I'm well financed. You've got the paperwork. My credit's great and the bank is offering an excellent rate on a business loan should I need it."

She held up her hand to stop me. "It's not your finances we're worried about. We don't know how you expect to make a living just selling fancy coffee drinks to tourists. You're probably not familiar with the lack of commerce on the West End. Sedona's not exactly a blue-collar town that needs a tradesmen's lunchroom."

I was shocked. She was talking down to me and belittling my project.

"The proposal explains it is planned to be an upscale café, not the run down sandwich shop that exists there now," I said.

"Do you clearly understand that we require a personal guarantee of full payment of all rent due over the life of the lease?"

I just looked at her and did a quick mental calculation of three years of rent times three thousand dollars a month. With extra costs and increases, we were talking over $110K. I put on my best game face but inside my blood ran cold.

"Of course, my counsel will have to review all the paperwork," I said.

"I understand you have some deep considerations here," she answered. After a long awkward silence, she shuffled some papers nervously and proclaimed, "I'm not even sure Mr. Stein will lease the space."

"I am. He wouldn't have agreed to this meeting if he wasn't interested in renting the suite," I replied.

"I don't think…"

"No, you obviously don't," I interrupted. I rose, collecting my papers. "I'll have to get back to you next week."

"I'll tell Mr. Stein we can't come to terms," she stated.

"No, you tell Mr. Stein I'll only deal with him from now on. I fully expect to close on this property." I took a few steps toward the door and stopped to add, "Oh, and I'll be e-mailing him that message as well, so make sure you don't get confused and tell him something else. That's how professionals work."

I left her office to discover my professional partner tossing cheesy popcorn into Moonbeam's mouth from across the room. I motioned for him to follow me and he quickly leapt to his feet, scampering after me.

As that first cold-blooded meeting ended, I carried my folders of papers and the contract home to ponder whether I would anty up or pass on the deal. The cold front howling in from the Northwest had crossed the Grand Canyon making ice cube snowflakes that stung my face as I left the office building.

Chapter 10

ALL DURING LATE MARCH and into early April, I stayed on the fence over the decision to sign. The expenses for permits and applications were negligible. I could step back at any time. If all the cards fell into play and I committed to the three-year lease, then it would be for the run of my life, no holds barred.

What kept bothering me was the personal guarantee; I couldn't afford to fail and then find a new renter to occupy the space. No, every dollar to my name would be wrung out of me. I would be ruined, destitute, finished. It was a major learning experience in business itself to meet with the various officials: a lawyer, bankers, and contract laborers who were needed at every step.

It was the conditions of the three-year lease and the

attitude of the landlord, the Stiller Group, and namely building owner, Bernard Stein, who had me on the razor's edge of scraping the project of acquiring the coffee shop in the beginning. Mr. Stein was a no-nonsense, inflexible attorney whose wealthy wife fell in love with the building and had to add it to her personal trust, allowing her real estate mogul husband to manage it. After years of losses and right-offs, Stein was determined to get the mausoleum opened up, rented out, and off his back.

There were no negotiations, just hard cold edicts and a twenty-page shopping center lease and the personal guarantee that demanded $110,000 over the length of the lease. Whether I lived, died, ran out or left my money to the kids, Stein would be paid first. When I protested and questioned this condition, Stein would not budge; take it or leave it, period.

I explored that prerequisite for anxiety-filled weeks by calling on other business owners, a lawyer, and commercial real estate agents. I put off the signing until July 1st, a full five months after our first introduction. Deep down, I was afraid of the clause and I just filed it away believing that Fate would be on my side. I hated that condition as it was as deadly as a guillotine hanging over my head. I blame the exhilarating weather, the unstoppable scenery, and the balmy wind for swaying me to sign on the dotted line that beautiful July day as I rode north through the Canyon toward Flag.

In my research I found out other commercial real estate brokers required the personal guarantee as many businesses were locked up and abandoned after a few months. In particular, Santino Carluchi gave me a brief and colorful account of the run-outs. Santino responded to my phone inquiry and reinforced that a separate agreement or a surety bond was required on every commercial rental he listed.

"So where ya' thinking of opening up your business," he asked via the phone.

"Corner of Dry Creek and the Highway," I said.

"Yeah, great location, don't know why there's a turnover there, town just hasn't gotten that far west," he said.

"In your opinion, is there any way to negotiate with the owner to omit the guarantee?" I asked.

"Nah, we all ask for the guarantee because so many new owners just disappear after six months. They couldn't make a go of it," he said. "They just run out in the middle of the night."

After the call to Carluchi, I knew my research on the subject of the personal guarantee was closed.

With the frequent visits to Sedona, a new awareness was in the forefront. The fact of living in the area was becoming the compelling force much more than the creation of a new business. Each trip to Sedona made leaving harder and the reality of being there full time became sweeter and sweeter. The pull was undeniable and strong. I just filed the inescapable requirement away and interred the personal guarantee deep in a stack of papers for later review and a much later decision.

The phone was ringing as I unlocked my door and ran into the entryway. It was April 20th, a full three months since first considering the acquisition of the coffee shop and a long six weeks since submitting all my information to apply to become a renter with the Stiller Group at the Dry Creek Plaza.

The caller I.D. indicated the Flagstaff number of the landlord's office and I cleared my throat to render an official greeting.

"Hello, this is Resa."

"Hello, Resa, this is Moonbeam calling from Mr. Stein's office at the Stiller Group."

"Yes, Moonbeam?"

"I have good news. Your application to rent Suite A at the Dry Creek Plaza has been approved," she stated.

"Thank you very much," I responded.

"Of course, we will now require your signature after you approve the lease and we will need your deposit of the first and last month's rent plus additional fees for the first month of CAMS."

"CAMS?" I asked, searching my memory for the full meaning.

"Yes, common area maintenance," she said.

"I understand," I replied. "I'll call to make an appointment for the signing."

A quick mental calculation made me realize the down money needed would be about seven thousand.

As I hung up the phone, I realized it had taken over six weeks to come through the approval process; the limbo was over. In spite of wanting to share the news with Barry, in my heart, I was still uncertain that I would ever sign.

◆◆◆◆◆◆◆◆◆◆

Later that evening, as I knocked on Barry's door to share the news from Flagstaff, I noticed some mail and packages at his door. I picked them up to hand them in as he answered.

" It's Merry Christmas, trick or treat, or a lottery win," I joked.

"No, it's none of the above," he replied. "It's my birthday," he said as he took the mail from my hands. He looked glum.

"Oh, don't be sad, you're only getting wiser with each gray hair and wrinkle. So that's why you're being visited by the Pony Express."

"Let's just hope there's money in there," he scoffed.

"Well, I've got some good news, another birthday gift of sorts," I said.

"What?"

"Stein's office called today and the application for the lease has been approved!"

"Be careful what you wish for…" he grumbled.

"Hey, there are reasons to celebrate, Mr. Future General Manager. What are you in the mood for? The tangerine chicken at Jade Pagoda or the tandoori grill at the New Delhi Palace, my treat?" I said.

"Yeah, that's a good idea, let's go. It's just that not

only is it my birthday," he replied, "Today is also the anniversary of Hitler's birthday. Oh, and Resa?"

"Yes," I answered.

"It's also National Hemp Day and the Columbine anniversary."

As we left, I tried to perk up his spirits. "Did you know that Hitler was a strict vegetarian and a dedicated dog lover?"

"Don't care, he was still Hitler," he grumbled.

Chapter 11

A SECRET PACT EXISTED in my consciousness and in my actions over the commitment to open the business. I decided to move forward on every detail as though I would be the new owner of a coffee shop but held in reserve the right to abandon the project in the final hour. My ethics gave my emotions permission.

I had to approach the City of Sedona for its approval for a business license. Also, I needed to face the City about the application for the front signage for the new coffee shop. My heart was set on the design drawn by Hoover years ago, the Weathervane: the nude man, woman, and flying horse. I took Barry along to shore up my fortitude and submit my application for the sign.

Sedona is nature's paradise and on record as a Dark Sky

City. Since the Big Pluto Telescope is housed nearby at the Lowell Observatory in Flagstaff, it is of utmost importance that glaring lights be prohibited. The requirements for signage are clear and specific about colors, designs, and lighting. The lighting had to be of low wattage and pointed downward on the new sign.

My sign would be simple. The design was art: man, woman, horse. Art is one thing that is respected in Sedona, a city that loves a work of virtu. From a pioneer woman in front of the library to the cowboy and Native American bronze sculptures in Uptown, art is everywhere. Even the bejeweled javelinas on display in Uptown are patterned in crazy quilt configurations and studded with semi-precious stones. They amuse the tourists and kids play magic with them for a few minutes.

The City's stipulations were formal and to the point with the instructions. My paperwork was complete with a copy of the image included. However, after waiting out in the City's zoning office lobby for a half hour, I heard unmistakable muffled snickers, giggles, and laughter coming from within the inner sanctum.

Barry was engrossed in a copy of *Mad Magazine*. I was squirming, growing nervous over the mirth coming from the distant office. Barry kept chuckling from time to time. On both fronts I heard laughter, a stereophonic effect, only this wasn't funny. The result was that my stomach twisted in knots and my nerves were raw with worry.

"I had no idea that outlandish magazine was still in circulation," I elbowed him a couple of times. "I read that when I was a kid, maybe ten years old," I remarked to deaf ears. The Howdy Doody face was still grinning at the world.

"World War II or the Fifties?" he asked. He got a very dirty look in reply.

"Well, my dear, it'd do you a world of good to relax and laugh more," he said, looking over the top of the rag.

"Guess I've had a lot on my mind, all these endless details. I can't even find an acceptable paint color for the sign in all these charts," I blabbered.

"Keep looking," he muttered.

Mr. Jared Axelrod, City Coordinator in charge of Zoning and Design, finally appeared. Along side Axelrod was an administrative assistant. She was a short, gray-haired woman with a flowered dress and a Barbara Bush-like figure. Her name tag read: Mildred. It was a comfort to see that Mildred hadn't morphed her name into an astrologic sign or a scientific term. She had a pair of bifocals hanging from a chain around her neck. Skittish as a newborn colt, I trotted back up to the front counter at full attention.

"Madam, I'm a bit worried about the figures on your sign," Axelrod told me.

"I believe the stipulations are all in order, the dimensions fit within legal code," I explained.

"No, I mean the figures."

"Oh, of course, the figures. Well, I've itemized the expense of materials and labor. So the figures should be accurate."

"You don't understand. I'm talking about the human figures depicted on the sign," he said.

"Yes?" I questioned with the same innocent expression I used when caught stealing mom's cookies as a child.

He held a drawing of the sign in front of him and clarified, "They appear to be nude." Mildred put on her bifocals and examined the picture over his shoulder.

"Mr. Axelrod, will we have to organize a Sedona feasibility study on this matter?" she asked. She gave me a look as if I'd been brought in on prostitution charges. She then rushed off to a nearby desk where she pointed in my direction and spoke in hushed scandalous tones.

"Yes, they're nude alright," he reaffirmed.

I took the drawing from him and looked closely proclaiming, "My gosh, you're right but I never thought of it that way. They are nude."

"Both of them," he added.

"The horse is nude, too," said his assistant. She'd returned with a bevy of elderly prim and proper clerical workers determined to investigate this atrocity at hand.

"I don't know how I could have missed that," I offered. As I spoke, the assistant reached over Axelrod's shoulder and ran her hand over the male figure in a slow seductive manner. Axelrod slapped her hand lightly and pulled the image from her. I looked to Barry for help but he was engrossed in his silly comic book, chuckling to himself. Where he was, when I needed him, was far away in a place for lost boys.

"Well, it's quite obviously a study in the unadorned,"

he said in a slow, direct manner.

"The horse is embellished with a breast plate," I ventured.

"The breasts, well, that's another area of concern," he said.

Hoping to gain some leniency, I suggested, "I believe they might be biblical figures. In fact, I'm sure of it. They're depictions of Adam and Eve."

"That can't be," said the assistant. In every Bible I've ever seen, they're wearing leaves. These people don't have any leaves."

Out of desperation I said, "Maybe this is done in the fall, you know, how the leaves fall in autumn?" That enticed a gasp of indignant disgust from the clerical worker and a half smile from Axelrod.

The group surrounding Axelrod had grown now. It seemed my disgraceful art was the most excitement this office had seen in quite a while. One of the office workers said, "Mr. Axelrod sir, there's no excuse for this. If God had wanted people naked, he would've made them that way." He responded by giving me a disbelieving look.

"You have influence with the committee. What are you going to tell them?" asked another.

"Yes, exactly what are you going to tell them?" asked yet another.

This was getting embarrassing, I thought. As they all continued to clamor for an answer, I leaned forward and asked softly, "What *are* you going to tell them?"

Axelrod smiled and slid the drawing back into its

manila folder. "I'm going to tell them the late artist, Hoover, was a genius. The city will be blessed to have more art like this." He gathered up the array of sheets, tapped them into a neat file and turned back into the interior of the office. We were dismissed.

"Well, how'd you think we did?" Barry asked, as we exited the City Office compound. The buzzing of the honeybees flittering among the purple desert sage blooms flooded my ears.

"We.... we......we?" I answered accusingly, as my voice lilted upwards.

"Don't speak French in public, it sounds so snobbish. How'd we do?"

"Well, we would've done much better if we'd both been in the room."

"You're right," he laughed. I should've been in there to make sure things went well. I got caught up in some childhood memories. Good literature can do that," he said.

"Literature, it's *Mad Magazine*, not *Macbeth*. Somewhere in between *T.V. Guide* and *Pro-Wrestling Weekly*."

"Culture snob. Wrestling is broadcasted on educational networks," he said.

"Where?" I asked.

"Idaho, where I planned a romantic getaway for us at the elegant Motel Molde de Spore," he joked. "That's off now."

"Maybe it's better you were quiet during the meeting."

"Okay, that problem is solved. How do you think we did?'

"It's hard to tell. Axelrod seemed to appreciate the intrinsic art value. But the committee has to vote on it. We'll be rejected for moral, offensive or suggestive reasons."

"So we can expect to be executed, excommunicated, or just plain asked to exit. So we do have options," he said.

"We need a plan 'B' and an approved color. How about this one?" I asked as I held up a swatch.

"Is that fuchsia?" he asked.

"No, not really, more a grape," I said.

He turned into Groucho, hunched down, taking long strides, puffing and wagging on the imaginary cigar, saying, "Well, in the fuchsia, please call it blueberry to avoid the confushia."

As he strode off from me, a passerby chuckled and called out, "I think he's getting away from you."

I shrugged and said, "I should've brought the leash."

Chapter 12

IN SPITE OF ALL the hundreds of details, the stress, the pressure and a major move, there were many wonderful discoveries becoming part of the day-to-day life in Sedona. It was a venture into new friendships and contacts. So many distinctive personalities reside by their personal choice in the valley of garnet colored formations and my encounters with artists, writers, the retired celebrities, the avant guard as well as unconformable characters grew daily. A variety of souls congregated here in Sedona magnetized by the pull of the Vortex.

Being surrounded by a banquet of stimulating world-class art everywhere I looked was a glutton's pleasure of visual stimulation. My soul fed on the beauty. The slab stone monoliths of the scenery turned Mother Nature into a teenaged party girl, whose face was heavily rouged and who showed off her finest couture designs fashioned in shades of cinnabar and scarlet.

In advance of the eminent rainstorm, the wind carried a flinty mineral smell that was mixed with a skunky juniper tinge. Rippled curtains of virga decorated the theatre wings of a stage set in red limestone. The thunder was rattling along the rim and already drenching the cloudland reverie high on Mingus Mountain. In a few minutes, hot flat drops of dust-laden rain would splat in a loose scattered pattern before the boomer broke loose.

The cloudbursts were frequent in the monsoon months and kept the tourists in their rooms at the resorts. Card games, board games, and naps replaced the sightseeing adventures. The dining room at the Weathervane Cafe was empty except for a few hikers and a couple sitting in mid-court, centered over the gold diamond-shaped star.

"Who are those two? Why do they look familiar?" I was motioning toward a well-dressed, older couple. I was whispering to Barry as he kept track of the written orders, lined up above the make table. He was watching our star food-assembler, Gerry, making sure everything matched up and then double and triple checked.

"They look familiar cause, Pumpkin Pie, they've been in here everyday this week," he answered. "They love your food."

I gasped and blushed a little, for a moment, speechless. "How do you know?"

"They told me, silly. They vacation here every year

and decided to have their lunch here every day on this trip. They're eating their way through the menu," he explained.

"Really?" was all I could counter.

"It's true, Resa, people love your food."

"Your food could make a vegetarian order veal and a steak man have a salad," he told me.

Suddenly Gerry stopped putting a dish together and stepped forward to enter the conversation. "He tells you the truth. I hear good things from people everyday."

Barry got uncharacteristically serious and added, "We're not kidding, Resa. It's the taste, presentation, and variety. That's a whole lot more than people expect from a corner coffee shop and café. You should be proud. Folks are talking about it all over the town. It's those three words you stressed so much when we started this."

"Back to work?" asked Gerry.

"No, 'word of mouth,' " Barry answered.

I choked back a little hiccup of surprise and felt my eyes well up with unexpected emotion. After all the months of preparation, hard work, and anxious anticipation, this was the first real affirmation. I'm not an egotist but I needed to actually know that my tension headaches and aching muscles might be at least partially justified.

"Hey now," consoled Barry with an arm around me. "Don't go getting all emotional on us. Remember guys only cry when they lose at poker or get hit in the bean bags with a line drive, if you know what I mean. Besides, Cream Puff, I think you put your sex appeal into your food." He tried to nibble my ear.

I went into that instantaneous switch from a tear to a giggle.

"You're chi, your attraction, your *vie de vie*", Barry went on.

"Oh, Barry, It's *joie de vive*," I muttered as I wiped my nose and eyes.

"That's right," echoed Gerry. "Don't go getting queery-eyed on us."

"He's been learning English from cable TV. He means teary-eyed," Barry told me. "The other day he told a customer he had to throw another shrimp on the 'Malibu Barbie.'"

Gerry went back to his work. He had become our star food-assembler. Although Barry referred to him and his brothers as 'Los Tres Stoogios,' Gerry took great pride in his work. We watched as he carefully and quickly placed all the portions on each plate with the precise presentation I'd taught him. He rarely had to look at the sandwich diagrams I'd drawn and hung above his station.

With thoughts back to the old couple, I said, "Send both of them desserts, compliments of the owner, please, Barry. Make it the prickly pear cheesecake."

I retreated into my retail alcove to busy myself dusting the items or "chochkeys," as Barry called them. After a buying trip to the Los Angeles Mart and the Chicago Mercantile Mart, my gift corner was filled with treasures for the tourists. I reasoned that they needed to carry home a small thank-you for the neighbor left behind who fed the cat and watered the plants. My shelves held kitchen gadgets, coffee and tea accoutrements, tinned cookies and candies, and several select gourmet items. There were gifts for the young and old, male and female. My best friend, Sissy, helped me assemble a number of gift baskets in various sizes with a nice range to meet the budget. They were ribboned in purple, tented in cellophane, and labeled with our gold seal. The baskets all contained a smattering of the items offered on the shelves. Grant, my youngest waiter, interrupted my dusting and positioning of choice items.

"Roland's here to see you," he informed me.

A little tickle of interest snapped me out of my trance. It had been a blissful few minutes of peace and quiet. I smoothed my hair, rubbed my lips together hoping for a smudge of color and wrenched off my food splattered apron. Roland was the Big Enchilada with the hulking food supplier Make-O. I was told they serviced only the large pricey accounts and that I was darn lucky they gave a small coffee shop the time of day. Many months ago my initial meeting with Roland was both a consultation and a learning experience. The start-up order to stock the shelves was based on the menu's needs and an empty pantry. The order was huge, took several hours to hammer out, and Roland had been a patient coach.

He stopped by occasionally to check on the account, sorting out problems and delivery errors. He was the only person I came in contact with who knew food, wine, and the finer things in life. While every other person who needed to meet with me had some problem or was selling something, Roland was someone I started looking forward to seeing.

"How's it going, Resa?" He was dressed in a three-piece suit and wore a touch of lavender cologne.

"Not too bad, Roland, nice to see you," I even managed a smile. He had a brown kraft paper wrapped bundle in his hands tied with chef's twine.

"I've brought you some wild rice from my personal cache until your order comes in," he remarked, handing over the package.

"Oh, how nice of you," I was sounding just a bit like a teenage kid at a charm school lesson.

The register on his voice lowered a little, "I wanted you to have enough for the chicken and wild rice soup. No on ever makes that anymore and it is delicious, Resa."

The package weighed about five pounds; I was both flattered and flabbergasted.

Roland was polished, refined and classy. He was always serious with a sensitive yearning in his eyes. He had been a talented food-smith who had been in the finest kitchens working his way up and up, higher and higher, until he commanded the acclaimed *L'Auberge's* back of house. He had been an inspired artisan chef until becoming the top local representative of Make-O.

As successful as Roland was in his career of fine food, he had been a failure with love. It was the map-like complexion of deeply pitted skin that made ladies decline his invitations in his younger years. Now in his early fifties, he had grown comfortable in a distinguished look but had given up on romance. Food and wine filled the gap.

I was probably blushing just a little and I stammered an appreciative, "Thank you so much," touched by his consideration, thoughtfulness and memory.

"Are you hungry, just a taste of something maybe? I've got a delicious green- herbed mayonnaise I just made or how about a pot of hot chili chocolate? Sorry about my humble offerings, not gourmet, but today's red chili beef sandwich is excellent." I was trying to tempt him with something a little distinctive.

"You really added a pot of chocolate Mexican-style to the menu?' he asked. Maybe I had sparked his interest.

"Slightly thickened, mysteriously curious," I described.

"All right, but please make it 'to go,' and include a spoon," he said.

"Right!" I hastened to the back of the counter secretly thrilled that Roland would touch anything at all of my creations. As I handed him the chocolate pot, he spooned a hot rounded, shiny blob into his mouth and rolled his eyes to the ceiling and smiled back at me. Then he was gone. I was pleased.

Just then the phone rang; it was late for a phoned-in or faxed lunch order. Gordon, the eldest of the three Filipino brothers, let me know it was for me.

"Hello, this is Resa," I spoke into the phone.

"Mom, it's me, Lacey." Of course, I could tell my daughters apart instantly. "I'm coming to Sedona," she announced without fanfare.

"What do you mean, a visit, Hon?" I asked quickly, thinking of work schedules, airport runs, the next day off or a partial day off.

"No, Mom, you're working so hard and I'm so over New York. I'm moving back to help you with the café. You're working too hard; I saw it last time I was there." She was determined.

"Oh, baby girl, are you sure?" I was giving her some room.

"No problem, Mom. I'll be there in about ten days and I already have a full-time job at the best spa in the world," she boasted.

"You mean the Miamo at the Enchantment?" I gasped.

"Yup, your daughter's already hired and on the staff. But I'm coming to Sedona to help you; you've been so stressed," she sympathized.

"Sweetheart, I can't wait. Call me. Do you need me to pick you up at the airport?" I asked.

"No, Mom, I have a surprise. Jimmy's coming, too. We're gonna try to live together; we're getting serious. Mom, I think he's *Mr. Right*."

"Jimmy? The Jim I remember from high school, that Jimmy?" My surprise was evident.

"Yeah, isn't it great," she was laughing. I was laughing too; we were joyous. Sometimes, something feels just great!

Back in high school, ten years earlier, Lacey and Jimmy had been an item for a long while. He was long, lanky and had that seventeen-year-old yearning saddled with a helplessness that some money, experience, and a vehicle would cure. Jim's longing for Lacey's company was undeterred by the lack of a car. The slim, tall young man surprised motorists who saw his knee-high jog, his black overcoat flapping like vulture wings behind him as he pumped along the three-mile trek from the village to our house.

He would worship Lacey, as everyone else did because she was sweet as honey, the genuine article. Everyone loved Lacey, always had, and Jimmy had a lot of competition mostly from their respective untested futures. Colleges in different parts of the country pulled them apart. The whirlwind of their freshman year inadvertently caused them to loose touch. Jimmy never forgot his first love; he carried her birthday date around as the PIN number of his life. He went on to become Captain James Forester, Pilot. Lacey turned to holistic medicine after getting her BA. A ten-year class reunion brought them face-to-face again and Jim was more deeply in love than ever. Transportation, money, and self-gratification were no longer hurdles.

"Mom, you don't understand how wonderful it is to be with someone you've known half your life, someone who knew the name of your old dog…who knows all about you and who's been to your house." She was making sense.

"Isn't life something, Honey," I answered. Maybe this was going to be a quality trial run.

"We're driving in. Can we stay with you until we get an apartment? I already have leads from the Internet," she asked.

"Sure, Sweetheart."

Now I was excited.

"See you soon; we're packing up two places. Be there end of next week. Got to go. Love ya!" Lacey was off and running.

As I put down the phone and turned, Barry said, "Oh, by the way, there's a message here. The City called today about the design for the outdoor sign."

Now I was at full attention and eager to know if the images of the unclothed couple would pass the surveillance of the Zoning Committee or a new look, name, and design would be needed.

"So Barry, what did they say?"

He let me stew a moment before revealing the decision.

"Axelrod said you can use your art if you airbrush the nipples and the aurora off the female figure."

"You mean the areola? A-R-E-O-L-A!"

"That's what I said, the aurora." Barry was now chuckling. "Yeah, Axelrod said, no nipples, no aurora!"

Chapter 13

GRADUALLY, LIFE AT THE coffee shop took on its own routine punctuated by the small vignettes of the repeat customers, the daily drama of the staff and my ever-changing schedule at the medical clinic.

"So how did everything go today, Barry," I asked, as I bustled behind the counter, expecting his daily update. The background music was crooning out *My Foolish Heart*.

"The Weathervane Café, my little Cheese Blintz, has become a meeting place."

"Who was in today?" I was interested.

The air was perfumed with toasting Saigon cinnamon aromas coming from the baking cooking dough I had prepared earlier and now entrusted to Grant to finish. He was eager to learn recipes, secrets and techniques, slowly becoming a prep assistant.

When the three brothers crowded around me, inhaling the fragrance of a big simmering batch of something meaty, they related their own food memories of their mother's homemade dishes. Gordon, Gerry and Grant drooled, recalling the diminutive woman, Tika Greenly, who had been a registered nurse, struggling to bring up the boys and immigrate to the U.S.A. After reminiscing about pork, noodles and rice dishes with names like adobo, palabok and bibingka, they usually checked in with her by phone.

"When we was kids, we worked in the cane fields all day long and followed our noses home to the good food smell from our mother's cooking, Resa," Gerry related.

Smiling, as if transported on the memory of the aroma of simmering pork, onions, tomatoes, peas, and garlic, Grant added, "It was always soooo good."

"She was the best cook in the village. Everyone wanted her recipes," added Gerry.

"When she cooked her lumpia with sweet potatoes we always had a relative or neighbor stop by," said Gordon.

"That was no accident," said Grant.

"I've had ukoy many times in restaurants but never as good as Mama Tika's," swore Gerry.

"She knows how to make the shrimp patties crispy and hot, juicy and firm on the inside," said Gordon as all three hummed in agreement.

"Some restaurants make the ukoy taste like tuna on styrofoam," laughed Grant.

The boys began to become hypnotic with the string of

memories.

"I just love her deep fried baby snakes. No one can serve up a plate of crispy fried snake like her," reminisced Gordon. They all agreed as Grant added, "Oh, my mouth waters when I think of her stuffed bull frog."

"The big ones are the best," said Gordon.

It was time to put my foot down when Gordon mentioned stuffed frogs and other reptiles as I noticed that the customers had stopped eating and were tuned into our conversation.

"Time to break this up, guys," I said.

I gave a gentle nudge to Gerry's shoulder in the direction of the prep line. They chatted to one another as they went back to their tasks. As I looked into the dining room, I saw a number of faces staring blankly at me, frozen in place from eavesdropping into the less than appetizing conversation.

"Of course, that will never be on the menu," I announced. "You do know that, right?"

Everyone chuckled and heads dropped back to the plates in front of them. I returned to the sink room to continue asking Barry of any more developments and to get out of view of the clientele.

"Oh and by the way," Barry drew out the word as long as he could in his broadcast announcer voice, "Our Honorable Mayor Puckett will hold the Mayor's Coffee Klatch here next month. The Inter-Galactic Space Travelers will now meet on the patio weekly. That means more coffee sales and the usual desserts."

"Great news!" I exclaimed.

"And Dipti and Ranjit traded out the sweets today and want to put a life-sized image of Dipti in the corner. What do you think of that?"

"Might be okay, I'll need to see it to know for sure," I deliberated. "A life-sized image of an imitation Eastern Indian woman in robes standing in the corner..."

"Holding a tray of her 'Dipti's Delectables,' don't forget," Barry said.

"That could give everyone the jitters," I said.

"It'll be here tomorrow. That Ranjit is just amazing. Seems he was a refrigeration technician in his former life before the ashram and finding, Betty, I mean Dipti," he informed me.

"Amazing, how?" I asked.

"He can fix anything; the dripping water line, the filters. He adjusted the hot water heater and all for a bowl of your chili," he explained. "Can that man eat...he's a regular Ralph Norton."

"What do you think they do with those stale cakes, Barry?" I was thinking recycling and makeovers.

"They toss them out at night behind their bakery. The wildlife loves them," he explained.

"Is that legal?" I pondered. The Great State of Arizona had passed a law complete with a $300 fine for feeding wildlife.

"Don't know, don't care, besides, how you gonna get an animal to pay a fine?" he quipped.

"Do you think feeding the birds is against the law," I

gazed out our windows.

"Only if they're jailbirds, nuc, nuc. I think you should get back to work, my little Prune Ruehgula."

"Whatever you say, my dear, *Jambe de Mouton*." Barry puffed up a notch and looked pleased.

The cookies were done and after loosing several large batches of expensive dough to inattention to details, such as time, temperature, and correct size, the snickerdoodles came out fine this time. The customers inhaled the homemade oatmeal raisin cookies, the chocolate chip cookies, and the chewy brownies we offered. The coffee shop fare would endorse the favorites.

Sales were a constant concern and nightly Barry and I went over the day's take.

We had a daily, weekly, and monthly bottom line. Both of us knew that the three thousand dollar monthly rent was the biggest hurtle we faced. In addition to that, we were charged a separate bill for the common areas. And no matter how tasty the chilies, the cold sandwiches, and the burritos were, it was the sales that walked in the door that ruled our business. My medical clinic paycheck was supplementing the monthly shortfalls.

"Are you listening, Resa?" Barry questioned me. "Will you place some ads in the *Red Rock News*, the hotel guide and the local radio station?"

"At the prices on this rate card, it's a 'no' to radio. We're not swimming in profits," I said.

"So I won't be hearing my partner on the transistor? F.M. could stand for 'fine meal.'"

Barry had a good brain for business and he was even better at spending my money. The underlying question was the practicality.

"What does a thirty second ad cost?"

"Spots are $25 each if we buy at least $200 a week," he told me.

"Let's check that math," I said.

"Sure, you can't ride the bus if you can't afford the ticket; you could buy me a ticket even if I'm broke. Or I can buy my own ticket and skip the ride. If you don't buy a ticket you can't win the jackpot. Or maybe we just miss the bus entirely and…"

"Barry!" I said, bringing him up for air. I picked up a slice of the apple pie from the display case. "We have to sell about sixty-six pieces of pie; about nine to ten slices a day to break even. Can we do that?"

"You are the wizard of the work week!" he said.

"I'm putting Lacey to task right away to do some marketing in the community," I said.

'Good, that way can reach some more people," said Barry.

"With me working two jobs and you here all day, I don't think we are out there enough."

"Speak for yourself. I'm plenty out there," he said.

"Not that way," I answered.

"That's a good point. I should join a club to get the word out. You know, meet potential customers," Barry said with a smile. "Internet dating, the Rotary, civic organizations... groups of foodies hoping to meet other foodies. Maybe I'll start a club".

"Oh, brother."

"No, listen, hear me out. How's this sound? Dates for dinner or partners without plates?"

"Sounds like a service for toothless people."

"Okay, how about meal mateys?"

"Pirates."

"Supper soldiers?" he asked.

"Too military, no one likes K-rations," I said.

"Café cronies, breakfast buddies, dessert doubles, friendly foods, or appetizer associates?" Barry tone was escalating towards frantic.

"Easy there, Cowboy. Don't get carried away."

"Yeah, it's not that important. " Barry switched off as quickly as he had started his rant. He turned to wipe down the counter. To answer, I just shook my head back and forth to indicate a "no." It was amazing to see how Barry could go on an outlandish streak as if it were a life or death matter only to blow it off in an instant. No matter what people thought about him, no one would ever say he wasn't interesting. His companionship was like a streaming, comedy show—sometimes confusing, sometimes annoying—but always entertaining.

Now getting back to the demands of filling the stomachs of the patrons, I was involved with two favorites: a hearty cold black bean salad and its first cousin, black bean cakes—totally vegan with no wheat. They would be offered as a burger or as a small plate with a garnish of a goat-cheese jalapeño sauce. I had given in to the gastronomic sensitivities of my clientele very quickly, after all, these weren't just matters of taste but health based choices due to a number of allergies and illnesses. So daily, the 'Specials' blackboard now noted 'no dairy, no sugar, no wheat, and meatless selections.'

"Mmmm, that tastes good!" Barry had dipped a clean spoon into the black bean salad for a quick, fly-in taste. "So will you buy some advertising?" he asked.

I was pouring the cilantro lime dressing in and tossing the vibrant green sauce over the raw veggies and beans.

"Really, Bar, word-of-mouth will bring them in."

"I want you to meet with the closed-circuit video people," Barry was worried and trying to convince me to spend precious dollars on advertising.

I smacked his hand as he dove into the salad for a second sample. With his mouth full, he replied, "It doesn't matter how many delicious items you plan for the menu. The only thing that really counts are the numbers at the end of each month."

"I'll think about it, but 'no' for now. Anything else?" I asked Barry.

"Yeah, we had some guys in here today who are raving about the fancy coffee drinks," he related.

"What kinda guys?" I asked.

"Well, let's just say...flamboyant," he quipped, "With the emphasis on flame."

"Oh, I get it." I said. Barry had an amazing memory for the details about the store's daily incidentals: the vendors, the record books, and our ever growing list of frequent locals. The cast of characters was growing.

"Well, I was behind the counter when they arrived," he began. As his tale began, I could imagine the scene in full Technicolor.

"Three men in their early twenties talking non-stop walked in, their hands and arms waving as if they were attempting flight. Each had bleached or streaked hair and some outrageous outfits, you know, colorful, bright and expensive. They took the table center of the room. I waited on them personally," he said.

"So, I say, 'I'm Barry. What poison can I disguise as food and sell you guys at inflated prices?'"

"Oh, Barry you didn't?" I groaned.

"They all giggled like school girls," he said. "So the tall slim one with bleached hair says, 'I'm Gene' and points to the one with eggplant colored hair and hoop earring and says, 'This is Dale.'"

"Yeah," I said.

"So, Dale introduces the third guy who has on a silk shirt opened down to his navel; he's complete with a tongue stud, and says, 'This is Sandy'. The eyebrows were wagging and they were actually flirting. I was shocked."

"You, shocked?" I asked.

"Gene says, 'Maybe you've heard of us, we're part of the local scene,'" Barry went on. So I reached over and grabbed a copy of the *Visitors Guide* and tore pages out looking for their pics. They howled. Then I told them, "Once I had a dream about you after being away at sea in the Navy for a long, long time."

"No, Barry, you didn't," I pleaded.

"They loved it. They laughed and squealed," he answered.

"'Just having some fun with you. Why—would I have heard of you guys? Are you famous?'"

"'Well,' Sandy says, 'in some circles we are.'"

"Resa, they were so raunchy and funny," Barry said.

"'Well, I can't imagine what for.'"

"They fell all over themselves with rib poking and snickers," Barry related. "So when I took their order, Sandy asks, 'What do you suggest?'"

"'Twenty years of therapy and a stronger father image,' was my answer."

"Oh, no!" I croaked.

"Relax," Barry said, "you'll love the next part."

"They actually clapped their hands and pursed their lips like adolescent teens to egg me on," he said. "So, I announced in my broadcast voice: 'Okay, boys, I have other customers waiting to see me. The main show starts at eight tonight with a two-drink minimum and a ten-dollar cover charge. Right now I'm headed back stage to return with three, very hot drinks I know you'll love. Don't beat up the pit boss, harass the keno girls, or heckle the next act while I'm away.'"

"You can't talk to people like that, Barry," I protested.

"They gave me a standing ovation and blew kisses at me. They'll be back soon."

I shook my head but asked anyway, "What did they have?"

"They loved the Red Rock Slide. One ordered that and one guy had the West Fork Trail blended with ice. I didn't say a word about the Tinkerbell with Fairy Dust," he confessed.

"Thank goodness," I said.

A separate menu with all the fancy coffee drinks was a playful expression of a fertile imagination and carried the names of local features and rock formations of the area.

I was in deep concentration chopping a three-pound jicama into julienne pieces readying it for a salad with Southwest tang and crunch while listening to Barry recount his latest story.

"And the last guy?" I asked. Slice, slice, slice, thin, thin, thin. The potato-like root tasted nutty and went well with the cilantro lime dressing.

"A Hot Chocolate Chai. They'll be back. Seems like this is a good place for a date." he said.

"Single's meeting place, coffee, and a first look-see. Humm," I answered. So the coffee shop was growing into that, too.

"Oh, by the way, the Sprout Kid was here today. Look at this." Two bursting bags tumbled out of the under-counter refrigerator. "I'm going to have Gordon garnish the dishes with these. Don't they look primo?"

I agreed as I helped myself to a sample of raw crunchy greenery.

"Sprout Kid?" I asked.

"Yeah, definitely a stoner," he analyzed with a big knowing smile. "Don't know what he majored in, but I'm guessing chemical dependency."

I just gave him a mean squint ending in a dismissive eye roll and went back to my knife work.

Since becoming a favorite, the black bean cakes were constantly in demand. They were made one of two ways, either by turning a three day old salad into a make-over or from scratch. I actually liked the end result but hated making them. They were popular as an appetizer or as a burger. It was the Teflon coated fry pan that did the trick of adding a crisp dry outer crust to the finished product after molding in cooking rings. The vegans, jocks, and yoga buffs who needed a light easily-digestible lunch ordered them in droves.

Chapter 14

I T WAS THE FAMILIAR radiology technician position that was hectic at times, yet the most orderly and peaceful part of my life since immersing myself in the Sedona food enterprise. I had become a registered x-ray technologist at the age of twenty and had always kept my hand in the profession. With marriage, children and homemaking, it was always the "go to" position; a fascinating field because the invisible becomes the visible. Sometimes I would be flippant enough to remark that I was an "internal photographer."

Since I specialized in Mammography for the last fifteen years, I was an advocate for the early detection of breast cancer and had always been involved with the Susan B. Komen Foundation and the Race for the Cure. Countless

113

luncheons of fowl had been offered at the fundraisers, the awards dinners, the fashion shows and the ladies' club meetings where the subject was research money for cancer in general or breast cancer specifically. A wave of aimless guilt, like an unearned pleasure, shrouded me after one of the more elaborate affairs, replete with canned lights, a master of ceremonies, a stage with runway, and expensive couture ensembles. Floral arrangements that mimicked a grand wedding seemed too rich for a group that promoted a goal to raise money for the fight against one of the scariest of diseases. I always hoped the flowers were donated and not purchased at retail in all their grandiosity.

The contrast of being literally out in the field working on a mobile unit that brought a fifteen minute mammogram examination to women wherever they lived and worked in the far reaching corners of the State was another world compared to the brightly lit and decorated ballrooms of the resorts where the galas were staged. I had met hundreds and hundreds of women; all ages, all nationalities and often thought that I could present a paper at a national conference documenting the ethnic differences in the breast anatomy, as different as their faces, of the world's women. The field of radiology was one that combined the science of physics and the art of photography. Whereas some of my fellow technologists disliked entering the darkroom to process their cases, I loved the sheer magic of the chemicals. The darkroom was the laboratory where the invisible was manipulated into a fixed image. The gurgle and hum of the machines replaced the hand tank method half a century ago and were a wonder in technology and speed.

As every technologist knows, each and every new box of film contains a creamy, stiff, white cardboard backing to protect the expensive x-ray film. And every tech took a few of these usually discarded cardboards home for their children's artwork and school projects. They were just too nice to throw away which was the ultimate end during times of department organization and inventory.

I found a use for them, too. On four of the 10" x 12" cardboards, I had drawn a draftsman-like reproduction of our sandwiches. It was both a picture and directions. They were taped above the make table to remind Gordon and Gerry the proper order of placement and ingredients for each sandwich. It was a drawing, a guide, and a constant reminder. Every three weeks, they needed a review when the Sonoran chicken sandwich, our best seller, came out with pickles belonging to the roast beef sandwich or the Chaparral ham sandwich came out containing spinach leaves and horseradish.

But smuggling several of the doomed to-be-discarded cardboards out of the clinic felt like heart-stopping, grand theft larceny. As the clock on the clinic wall neared four-thirty during my first week of employment, I tried to be nonchalant about spiriting the needed cardboards into my handbag. I dreaded being caught "stealing" the white cardboards. I was the new girl, a recent hire at the medical clinic, and I felt my throat tighten in a constriction of fear as I tried to smuggle the papers out.

"Time to go, Resa?" a voice behind me asked as the cardboards silently disappeared under my lunch tote.

I froze with alarm. "Yes, finished for the day," I said as I turned around to face the supervisor, Lisa. Luckily, she hadn't seen my theft.

"My room's cleaned up and the unit is shut down," I added. "I'm off to the coffee shop."

"Okay. Don't forget, Admin wants you clocking in and out no more than five minutes before and after your shift. No unauthorized overtime," Lisa said.

"Got it! See you tomorrow." I walked down the hall to punch out, hardly breathing, with guilt making me jumpy.

Second only to the constant employee drama at the coffee shop, consistency was the next biggest challenge and the cardboards would help with the problem of keeping the sandwiches coming off the line as clones instead of haphazard science projects. When I wasn't present to watch over quality control, the cardboard instructions helped to aid the staff. If the non-professional staffers, who had no food training, didn't put their own spin on the menu's offering, then the suppliers didn't provide the ordered ingredients. On Mondays the bread was always late. Tuesdays the produce man pawned off four-day old greens and on Wednesdays, the juice delivery lacked the favorite orange-mango blend. Essential for the vibrant green cilantro lime salad dressing, the quart of fresh squeezed lime juice would not be delivered mid-week, causing a hole to be filled by another salad as the customers pouted. If I ordered pastries and espresso coffee cake from the artesian baker, he arrived with some of his own selections instead of the anticipated items. In any restaurant the public wanted the same taste they'd grown accustomed to finding. Most weeks I was a juggler and a cook, trying to keep my loyal regulars happy.

Flavor is what we specialized in to set our taste apart from the ordinary. When you think of lunchtime being the perfect meal for a sandwich, you think of chicken, ham or beef, with chicken being ordered two to one over the others. After our initial stumbling in keeping perfectly fresh delicious bread and rolls for our sandwiches coming through the door daily, we had three savory sandwiches and often a fourth hot sandwich. That was usually shredded red chili beef with or without napolitos, a tenderly cooked edible cactus.

I was reminding Gerry, who had now been promoted to taking a turn at the make table, to assist when the rush became overwhelming for his older brother, Gordon.

As I taped my sandwich diagrams to the wall above the make table, I said, "You only need to follow the diagram. You see, you layer it from the bottom up. Doesn't that make sense? No guess work, make it *exactly* like the picture. Follow the instructions!" I waved my index finger in the direction of the stolen cardboards.

One distinguishing addition to the lunch lineup was that each wrap or sandwich was served enveloped in a thin, crisp, translucent purple paper meant to keep the contents neat and customers' fingers clean. The color-coordinated sheet was a big hit and each sandwich was cut open to reveal the stratified ingredients in a gift-wrapped package.

Gordon and Gerry nodded in agreement, but I knew there would be another repeat training soon in how to matchstick a purple onion and add just a touch, not more than eight or ten pieces total to a salad.

Barry handed me the phone. "It's your friend Sissy. She's not planning to be here again, is she?" he hissed.

"Hush!" I grabbed the phone from him.

The weight and pace of the coffee shop and the clinic job had consumed me and shut down any possibility for a social life. This was my life as well as my neck.

"I'm about twenty minutes away, just getting into Cottonwood. Can I come over and stay with you tonight?" she gushed. "I miss you, Sweetie. We need some girl talk."

There wasn't a brain cell left in my head to pay attention to the lighter points of fashion, make-up tips, or her latest romantic adventures. Sissy was a cougar on the prowl. She was beautiful, rich, and flirtatious. People loved her but often talked about her, too. She was an easy mark for judgmental criticism. Many were jealous that "play" was her full-time occupation. She was on her way to act for a short while as a waitress at the Weathervane Café and flirt with the cream of the crop male customers. She'd have a karaoke date for a drink and a song within an hour of donning an apron; that was my girlfriend, Sissy.

With my hand clasped over the mouthpiece, I hissed back, "Please, Barry." Sissy wasn't the only person I knew who dropped in for an hour or two, giving advice, offering their own knowledge, sometimes drying some dishes, or wiping down a few tables. It wasn't that I was unappreciative. I was. My commitment was total; Barry, however, had no patience for the visitors.

"Barry, she has our best interest at heart," I told him. Secretly, I wondered if my energy level could handle an evening visitor and an overnight guest.

When I first imagined and considered coffee shop ownership, I had mistakenly dreamed of the assistance of family members. If I had been in my thirties and had my group around me, the endeavor may have turned out differently; more like an Italian family, squabbling, cooking, serving, and running a store together.

Twenty minutes later, Sissy blew in. She was pure sunshine. She stopped to greet everyone and anyone in her path, even the strangers. She was perpetually smiling with a quick, cute laugh and a toss of her thick, blonde mane. She gave off the possibility that the right guy could get lucky. A few did and were loyal forever. She was a living love drug. To add to her credit, she was an exceptional home cook. She was just plain sexy about her whole aura as she was about her love life. As soon as she saw Gerry, who was bussing the remaining empty tables she sent him out to fetch something in her car. Barry was already grimacing.

"Are you Grant or Gordon?" she always confused the waiters, whose mother had chosen names starting with "G" on purpose—to go along with the sound and alliteration of their father's English name, Greenly. She really didn't know one Greenly from another.

"I'm Gerry," he was at attention, ready to please Sissy.

"Go to my car, the white Mercedes, and bring in the big box in the back seat and don't forget to lock it," she instructed, handing him her heavy key ring.

As she approached mid-room, she exclaimed, 'How stunning the gold diamond shaped star is, just right in the purple floor!' She gushed over how "YUMMY" all the serving platters, heaped with salads, looked in the chilled display case. Her perfume, a fragrance called *Joy*, arrived before her. She was slowly advancing toward the back counter spreading cheer to her admiring audience.

As she put down her *Louis Vuitton* bag, she endeared herself with charming banter to a complete stranger. Barry wagged a finger to beckon me toward him.

"You are such a pushover," he whispered, shaking his head at me.

"At least I still have a few friends, *Monsieur Coq d' Bruyere*," I snapped back.

Barry turned a shoulder and busied himself with communicating with the internal workings of the cash register.

The big bulky box contained a large capacity General Electric Dutch oven that could hold six gallons. Everyone gathered around while Sissy hosted the unveiling. Gordon was using one of my sharpest chef knives on the box. Now Barry had his back turned pouring himself a cup of sustaining brew, a bold Yirgacheffe. He was doing his best to ignore all of us.

"Oh, can I have one, too, Barry?" Sissy could be commanding, never realizing that others really didn't want to cater to her.

Barry sulked, but complied. "Will there be anything else, Madame?"

"No, Precious," she cooed.

"So what's this for?" he asked, handing Sissy our coffee cup, imprinted with the logo. She worked on her dark liquor, stirring in heaping spoonfuls of sugar and bringing the brew to a light tan color with ample cream. Barry winced with a look of horror at Sissy's liberal additions.

"Ah coffee...black as night...sweeter than love... stronger than death," he quoted.

Gordon asked, "What's this for, Resa?"

I piped up. "We need bigger amounts. We're going through the chilies and the shredded beef every other day. Now I'll make it in bigger batches and we'll freeze half," I explained.

Out of the corner of my eye, I saw Barry turn towards the windows and stare at the red rock views in the distance and shake his head back and forth in disapproval.

The conundrum of Matt Richard's "no kitchen" mystery was solved by plugging in a large electric hot plate burner and cooking our batches a kettle at a time. Now with many months of clients behind us, we ran out of the mainstays too quickly. They were made ahead and the crew just reheated the soups and stews. "No kitchen" meant that the former movie theater lobby had had a popcorn stand complete with a hot dog cooker. Matt had added the espresso machines and cold display cases, converting the area into his sandwich shop. The absence of an open gas grill, deep fat fryers, and a powerful vent meant "no kitchen" to a real chef. By adding electric appliances, a griddle and two microwaves, I was able to cook the tightly controlled menu. By heating cast iron platters in the oven, entrees could be served. Now I was ready to cook twenty pounds of red chili beef at a time or make enough green chili pork posole for a week.

Chapter 15

"Quick, I hear her coming, she's on the patio. Get ready." Barry yelled.

As he swiftly prepared my usual double shot caramel coffee drink, the staff hurried to lower the music and change it to one of my specified selections. They were crossing the line again, playing some of their head banger noise in my absence. I made a mental note to address the indiscretion to Barry who was clearly being permissive on the matter of way out popular trash over the goal of pleasant subtle background music. Through the windows, I could see a flurry of activity aimed at showing me they were all busy, productive, and happily awaiting my arrival. I was greeted by smiles, warmth, and puppy-dog looks from the youngest of the Filipino brothers, Grant.

The minute I crossed the threshold, an iced caramel *macchiato* was in my hand and all four men looked at me awaiting my approval. My radar told me told me this was a planned act, a male smoke screen, a set-up.

"Today I hired a new guy." Barry was in the middle of his daily news update of briefing me. We had been working seven days a week for many months, and we had the haggard look of street orphans. The average tasks of laundry and housecleaning were ignored until no longer avoidable and then done at manic speed. Both of us were short on sleep and eating at odd times. Keeping the energy level up that way was causing a noticeable weight gain. As the old adage goes, "Water, water, everywhere, not a drop to drink," and we found ourselves constantly thirsty. Even the fresh coffee, iced tea, bottled water, or prickly pear lemonade we set aside for ourselves remained untouched. In short, we were lethargic, grim, apathetic, and gaining weight. Barry and I each needed a clone or an assistant.

"So who's on board?" I asked wearily.

"Name's Ned. Just heard about the coffee shop through the grapevine and seems he's had some great experience in Seattle. Kid's got an outstanding resume. Here, take a look. If his resume were any better, I think we'd be applying to work for him."

It was another overly qualified candidate. The pendulum swung widely, under-qualified, over-qualified. I needed to hire one formally food-trained assistant to help me at least one day a week before my own personal meltdown.

With a gaggle of enlightened seekers of wisdom and a bevy of the wealthy, housing in Sedona was scarce and expensive. Consequently, the labor pool was thin. Possessing over a hundred professional kitchens, including the world-class resorts, our town was a magnet for talent. A good chef could name his own price. I didn't need that level of skill for my modest selections, just a sous chef who could slice a tomato or onion properly. I started calling the culinary institutes in Phoenix, but to no avail; a part-time position was not a plum of a job. At least Barry would catch up on his rest now that he had added an assistant manager. Lately, he hadn't been able to crack a joke.

Ned's resume showed experience in coffee and maturity, something lacking in each and every other employee who changed the specific directions or shirked common sense duties.

"So what's a guy like this doing here," I asked.

"Can't answer that one but he'll be here in an hour for your final stamp of approval," he said. "At least I haven't seen him on *America's Most Wanted*, so he's not on the run."

"So, anyway, are there any other things I need to know, Barry?" I asked. "There's a napolitos salad waiting for finishing touches and the tomato basil soup is ready to put in the cooler."

"I've gotten three complaints this week about cat hair in the cheesecakes. You've got to do something about your supply from your friend, Morgan. This is a café, not an animal shelter."

"I'll talk to her," I mumbled, hanging my head, paralyzed momentarily with fear and embarrassment over the destruction that a few bad comments around town could do to the reputation of cleanliness I fostered.

"Just quit taking them; you can bake a cheesecake," he advised.

"Of course I can, Barry, but I can't take on one more thing."

"Another bunch of locals have started to come in. It seems like a roundtable business meeting. You'll get a chuckle out of these guys and the Tin Foil Hat Lady is now on the horrors of electromagnetic waves," Barry laughed.

"I might have to disagree with her on that one," I said. Secretly, I believed a little radiation wasn't all that bad after all.

"Hate to tell you, but the ice machine is down. I sent Gerry out to bring in bagged ice till the repairman gets here," he shared.

"What's wrong with it?" I asked.

"Ranjit gave it the once over. That guy is a Picasso with pliers. He could fix the crack of dawn or a fractured skull. He's a Monet with a monkey wrench."

"All right, all ready! What's wrong with the ice machine?"

"All the years of neglect have clogged the pipes with minerals that are building up in the new filters we installed", he said.

"Any recourse with the landlord over his bad pipes?"

"Not a chance. Stein reminded me it was an "as is"

building. Practically laughed at me," he said. "The bad news is that our water filters on the espresso machines will go next if we don't install a special intake filter."

"What's the good news?" I asked.

"Ranjit will do it for chili," he said.

"So we better prepare for the worst. Maybe I'll send Stein a poisoned pen e-mail."

"Keep cooking. I'll feed Ranjit your chili till his eyes turn brown," added Barry. "Next on the agenda, Grant is asking for an advance on his paycheck. I caught all three of them pulling cubes of pork right out of your giant cooker when you weren't looking. They gobbled it hot and sizzling. Burned their mouths."

"No wonder that batch seemed light," I was rising out of my chair.

"Relax, they won't ever do it again," he said. "Oh, we had an incident earlier today."

"Oh, what?" I was scared to ask.

"Ah, one of the customers tore into his bowl of chili and, and, and…he was cracking up and telling jokes at the same time and…"

"What?"

Barry couldn't get it out. "After the punch line and his big booming laugh, he choked and, ah, ah, chili shot out his nose!" he chortled.

"Wha'd you do?" now I was laughing, too. "Call an ambulance?"

"Nah, handed him a dish towel!"

For the next few hours before work was done, all Barry

had to do was wave the dish towel to get me laughing again. He played up the chili incident over and over wearing a towel as a mask and flagging a red-colored towel in front of my eyes.

Somehow we were ready to leave fifteen minutes after close. We were getting into a routine, a groove. Barry turned to me and said, "I insist we have an outing tonight. We need a break, a night out. What you always look for—a great meal, the right music, a quiet alcove . . . we haven't laughed in so long."

"You mean we can still have some fun?" I was wistful. His antics had softened me and made me want some more laughter.

Barry was right. A few hours out of the coffee shop helped to ease the strain. After a superb meal at Mai Thai on Main Street in Cottonwood my appetite was content with flavors from tom ka soup, crispy golden paddles and a fragrant lemongrass chicken salad. My cravings would be abated for many days after the infusions of ginger, hot Thai chili, and coriander. Mai Thai served food distinctly from the Northern provinces near Laos. While I had enjoyed the ice-cold vanilla flavored, orange-colored Thai tea, Barry ended his dinner with the strong French coffee, slowly dripping through a metal strainer into the thickened, sweet condensed milk.

As the tinselly music chimed softly in the background, we talked about nothing special avoiding any discussion connected with the coffee shop.

"Psychiatrists say that if you're normal you have to

love yourself before you can love anyone else. Someone who doesn't like anyone is subconsciously unhappy with themselves," I mused.

"No, I have the exact opposite theory, he replied, "many above-average people try to improve through personal growth. Because they are so normal, they see the faults in themselves and the faults in everyone else."

In spite of being tired, I wondered where this was going: a set up for one of his punch lines or an actual thought process.

"Now," he continued, leaning forward for emphasis, "Since I'm normal I don't want to be reminded of my frailties, so I subconsciously dislike everyone."

"I guess that makes sense," I said.

"You see, because I'm so normal, I see me in them. I don't like what I see because I'm not content with who I am."

"You're not?"

"Of course, not. I'll only be content when I become what I want to be," he answered.

"When will that be?"

"I don't know. I haven't decided exactly what I want yet."

'So you don't really like anyone?" I asked.

"Oh no, I get along with just about everyone. You know that," he replied.

"But you just said..."

"That may sound like a contradiction but all the hate and self-loathing are on a subconscious level. I've never experienced it in real life," he explained.

"Then how do you know it's there at all?" I asked, half laughing.

"Because I'm so pathetically normal," he said with a straight face.

"Do you think so?"

I'm a prototype for normal. I'm so normal the Gallop Poll makes up their stats to match with me."

"Hey, let's get back before I fall asleep," I said. This was coming from one of the more unusual persons I knew or at least I thought I knew.

My head was seeking a comfortable spot on the backrest of the car seat as I could feel the pull of sleep coming on as we drove past the glow from Jerome.

"Look at the lights, Barry. They're twinkling like diamonds. Jerome is the tiara on the forehead of the night," I murmured, admiring the lights in the distance.

"Where'd you get that one?" Barry asked.

"Made it up," I said.

"You sound like a shaman," he remarked.

"No, look, Barry, the lights of Jerome are like sparkling gems. Maybe Sedona is rubbing off on me," I answered.

"Women will find any excuse to buy jewelry," he cracked. It was one of the lines he stole from his collection of comedy tapes.

Barry was in full comedy mode making us both laugh again. He had nailed one of Don Rickles' well-known lines. I knew he harbored a future wish to hold an open microphone night at the coffee shop where he could perform his comedy routines as a headliner to the musicians and poets that assembled to perform.

As we rode the long stretch of highway through the open Native American Indian land, Barry's mind was somewhere else. He was thinking about a spotlight where people lined up for a good seat and paid to laugh. Suddenly, Barry did a mental two-step and floated himself right out of the car. He was instantly transported to the same place he always seemed to go to escape whatever troubles crowded his psyche.

The small jazz trio finished an impromptu riff accentuated by a pop of the snare and the crash of the high hat symbol. At that precise instant, Barry jumped to center stage drenched in the white-hot spotlight. His 1950's styled sharkskin suit was just slightly brighter than his toothy smile as he assessed the front row. He flicked the ashes from his cigar with his right hand while pulling the mike and the stand with his left hand to his mouth like an Army sharpshooter preparing to take aim.

"Let's hear it for 'em folks. Gerry, Grant and Gordon, the 'Flipino Trio.' A finer bunch of felons I've never had the pleasure of working with. I'm kiddin', I mean it. I love these guys. But not in the way you're thinkin' pal."

Quickly turning, he addressed a neatly dressed man in the front row resembling a patron from the coffee shop.

"One of their cousins is from the capital of the Philippines, works as a contortionist. He's a Manila folder."

A shapely waitress in a short, tight outfit wandered in front of the stage with a tray of drinks. As she crossed the spotlight, he recognizes her as Sissy.

"Okay, folks, this is the telepathic portion of the act. Miss, I'm going to tell you your lucky number. I'm thinking of it now. 584-212-3…"

"That's my phone number," Sissy called out.

Barry announced to the audience, "You dial that number later, you're gonna get lucky." The audience roared its approval.

Out of the corner of his eye, Barry caught Ned sipping a martini and looking like a glassy-eyed zombie.

Barry took a puff off his cigar and moved in. "What's your name Skippy, got any idea?" Ned was caught off guard and didn't respond.

"Come on Steven Hawkins, they don't get much easier than this. I don't know how many of those Shirley Temples you've had tonight, but I guarantee they won't make you forget your own name. But then again, in your case, it might be a blessing."

The crowd applauded and Barry walked back to center stage. "Sorry folks, he's like my girlfriend, way too easy. I'm movin' on."

He was on his game and in his element. The crowd was his and the room was perfect. Sure it was just a Vegas show lounge. It wasn't the big hall. It wasn't the concert stage. But it was his. Tonight he owned it, and that combination of power and performance adrenalin was all he needed to satiate all his creative needs.

One table in, stage left, sat two women in stylish, low cut dresses. They drank cosmopolitans and mysteriously resembled Resa and another lady. He looked sheepishly down their dresses and stood silent. Expecting the barrage of punch lines, the audience giggled and chortled.

"I was just thinking...I gotta fly over the mountains tomorrow." The audience howled and he continued, "No, I'm serious. Aren't there four peaks in Reno? I don't know what brought that up? Of course, I haven't brought it up in a while, that may be the problem."

As if he had no idea of the innuendo he'd delivered, he leaned over the stage to talk to the ladies in question.

"Honestly girls, I have no idea what they might be thinking." As he spoke he pulled a string from inside his lapel. His tie slowly rose forward until he slapped at it like an embarrassed schoolboy.

Again addressing the women, he gave a fake apology attempting to reel them in for more easy laughs. "My God, I am so sorry. Have you ever seen anything like that before in your life?"

Without missing a beat, Resa responded, "What's that, a guy who get's caught up in his clothes and can't perform?"

The crowd loved it and applauded their approval. Barry grabbed his chest as if shot in the heart, and stumbled around the stage to milk the laugh.

"Oh, my heart. Right in the aorta. Who's idea was it to put Vampira in the front? Miss, if I knew you were going to show off, I'd of worn the bullet proof cummerbund tonight!"

As the crowd kept laughing, he knew it was time to wrap it up. Turning to the band, he instructed, "Okay, mi amigos, play us oughta here, quick before she reloads."

The band played, the laughs turned to applause, and Barry smiled to himself as he brought himself back to reality.

Barry slowed the car and turned down the lane. I had

fallen asleep as he played the lounge act in his imagination, a place where he was the star act.

"If you had been awake you could have had a front row seat to the show," he said as I started to rouse.

"Reese, wake up," Barry nudged me as we arrived at my place.

Startled and confused, I asked, "Is it time to get up for work?"

"No, you're home. Go on in and get a good night's sleep. You've got a full eight hours before reveille," he said.

As Barry pulled away after saying goodnight, he went over his lines perfecting his jokes, knowing I had missed his first-rate, crackerjack act.

◆◆◆◆◆◆◆◆◆◆

Next morning it was my turn to open up and start the large urns with the morning's fresh rocket fuel. Since I had several boxes to carry in, I took the back hallway into the coffee shop. Foremost on my mind was to have a cup of the first run of the fresh batch of the breakfast blend. I needed my number one jolt of hot, strong brew. What I looked for was the 'all right with the world feeling' to flow into my brain. It took several minutes to crank up the cauldrons and start to hear the steaming water flow over the nutty grinds. My empty cup was positioned under the spigot and I was ready to bleed off the hot juice even before the ready light indicated the batch had finished.

With the swiped coffee in hand, I rounded the bend past the front counter to unlock the glass doors and click on the open sign. Turning back with nose in cup, blowing and taking tiny scalding sips, I heard an ear piercing scream a long second before I realized that it was coming from me. I faced a human figure standing in the corner where no one was supposed to be. I was not alone and that split-second of fear took the hot coffee flying with a splat as I jumped backwards a few feet, gasping with shock. As instantly as I had been frightened to a heart-stopping jab, my anger took over upon discovering that the figure that ambushed me was none other than a cardboard likeness of Miss Dipti, of Dipti's Delectables, complete with a tray in her hands and a full line of sugarless cakes on display.

Nothing reduced the spinning out-of-control feeling I had, as I wiped up the puddles to remember in the fog, that Barry had briefed me that an Eastern Indian woman's life-sized image would now stand guard in the Weathervane Café.

Chapter 16

ON A GORGEOUS SUNLIT day, the coffee shop was filling up early as we opened. A back corner was soon occupied by the members of the Business Brainstormers, a loosely, self-organized bunch of men and women who inspired one another with future money making ideas. Their ultimate goal was to slowly discuss enterprises and someday choose one to back, in-force. As they arrived each week, the group grew in numbers and included people of all ages. Sometimes the Tin Foil Hat Lady and another of her anti-pollution followers, our local Feng Shui Master, Su Ling Chow, joined in the group. They were a happy, loud bunch always welcoming anyone who had an outlandish but workable idea.

They had a format which allowed each member time,

round-table style, and in a considerate order, to fully explain his or her personal concept. Robert's Rules of Order were not necessary. They always rearranged the tables to form an unofficial conference room and ordered the sweet desserts and gallons of coffee. Fueled by the sugar, alkaloids and caffeine, they were a jubilant bunch, racing on ideas and stimulants.

Lacey was assisting today, fetching coffees and keeping the group happy. Her cheerful personality was not only an asset to the coffee shop but also to the spa where she worked in Boynton Canyon.

"Mom, you should hear what the group's talking about; they've got some pretty cool ideas for the environment. They are so green."

"That's nice, Honey, but I don't have time right now." Involved in a vat of mango salsa for the crispy queso quesadillas, I was busy as usual chopping, mixing, and tasting to get it right.

Barry overheard the request from Lacey and butted right in. He took the spoon from my hand and stuck a freshly brewed cup of bold Kenya, laced with a drizzle of cream, into the open space.

"Go," he ordered. "Go over there and listen to them for a few minutes. Take a break. You'll learn something," he shooed me away. "Don't worry, I'll wrestle this into the cooler. Go now!" he insisted.

"Go on, Mom." Now Lacey was siding with him.

Bert was semi-running the meeting. He had an idea that he was just finishing up revealing. The others were making their comments and additions. I caught a little information as the members pushed open the line-up of chairs and gladly welcomed me. What I grasped of his idea was a concept that could apply to any start-up business.

"So, this saves or redirects the small time entrepreneur's budget," Bert was espousing his latest brainchild. "A franchised company sets up these production kitchens all over the country; we start in major cities first." The members murmured agreement and heads nodded. Lacey brought over a full pot of the steaming Kenya and centered it on the table for refills.

Bert turned to me and recapped. His look told me that he was flattered the owner had joined them. My customers now vied for a few minutes of talk or attention from me; I now knew the thrill of minor celebrity status.

"The company has bays with all the commercial equipment installed; the hoppers, bottlers, a canner, and labelers are provided. Of course, all the Health Department licenses are already in place," he said. All heads turned to me to see if I was getting it: the concept. I almost choked on my sip of coffee, snapping back to full attention.

"So, let's say someone wants to produce his mother's recipe for spaghetti sauce, or someone wants to test the market for a single serve, pre-packaged children's snack."

"Remember that crazy idea for bubble iced-tea a few years ago?" Neil interjected. "That one went belly up." His thumb pointed downward.

"Yeah," murmurs broke out; side talk started.

"They shoulda known that was a loser," Bert

continued. "With this concept, a person doesn't have to go out and buy all the equipment first just to find out that no one wants the spaghetti sauce. He rents a bay at the proving ground kitchen and launches his business after knowing it can fly!" Approval and nods followed clapping around the table.

"Fredericka, this could be perfect for your idea. Why don't you go next?" He sat back down.

Watery-eyed and raspy voiced, Fredericka, now the star speaker, rose to her feet. She rummaged in the canvas bag on the chair next to hers and produced a very professional-looking retail product. She arranged a number of items center stage, her hand trembling just a little. Every eye was on each bottle, jar, and small dish she lined up, one at a time. The business group was patient and rustled in excitement as Fredericka laid out her goods. She cleared her throat.

"Well, I've been doing this for years. I have a few clients and here's my idea," she stated. We all stared at her shakers, small wine bottles, and saltcellars, each one containing a vividly colored substance.

"I call my product *See Salts*, S-E-E-S-A-L-T-S, cause you can see, smell, and taste it. Actually, you can see how much you sprinkle on your food!"

"So, how's that different from other seasonings I can buy at the grocery?" asked Phillip, playing the antagonist.

"Glad you asked that question." The pat refrain made the group chuckle in unison and Fredericka continued.

"It is made by a secret solar process I patented. The

method retains the natural vivid colors, flavors and aroma of each ingredient. It's fresh and organic, *violá*"

There was a louder murmur as the group reassessed her line-up.

"If you think about it, all the seasonings you see at the stores are dried-out and brown," she said.

They now paid more attention to how green the multi-herb salt was. How deeply burgundy the fragrant, herbed, wine salt in its own split-sized shaker bottle appeared and now they focused on the open salt cellar. They were sniffing, inhaling the essential oils of rosemary, garlic and thyme and tasting each one. I shook a dash of Fredericka's wine salt onto the palm of my hand and tasted it. The connection started to light up the pathways in my brain between the mouth and the imagination. As I stood up and turned towards Gordon who was at the grill, he snapped to attention. Just then both Gerry and Grant alerted to the energy shift in the room.

"Gordon, beef loves salt! Sizzle two pieces for everyone here at the table. Heat up some chicken filets, too. Slice and grill some thick slices of onion. No seasonings. Grant, get some napkins and silverware for everyone. Gerry, please quarter up and seed six red peppers. Chop some 'cukes'! Hit the grill," I shouted.

"And Gordon, spin some raw sprouts, lettuce, and tomatoes and put them on a platter. Pronto! We're going to do a taste test of Fredericka's flavored salts."

The excitement around the table grew as the smells wafted from the grill during the short wait. A platter of raw vegetables arrived first and was a deconstructed salad, naked and unadorned. It consisted of spinach leaves, tomatoes, olive oil, and roasted red peppers. Lastly, Gordon delivered platters of hot, sizzled beef and chicken with thick onion slices accompanied by lightly grilled slices of our sourdough bread. The heavy dishes were passed from hand to hand, family style. I turned back to Fredericka.

"Please instruct us as we taste," I said.

The group's anticipation was as high as a gang of kids in an ice cream shop. Everyone had a sample of each item on his or her plate.

"The wine salt would be best for the beef," Fredericka said. "Of course, the green herb salt would be best on the raw vegetables. Let's all sample the Italian blend on the peppers," she suggested.

There was a chorus of "ooohs" and "aaahs" as everyone dug into the impromptu taste test.

"What's that?" Mandy asked, poking her finger at the flecks of bright colors in the very fine powdery salt in a decorative dish set table center. It smelled like mint and roses. Fredericka inhaled and rose up to her full height.

"My *piece de resistance*— it's a salt for weddings in the bride's choice of colors and flowers." Twittering and exclaiming "ahhaaa," the women at the table were more interested than the men.

"There are over seventy edible flower petals," she explained. "I can make any color of salt or make it multi-colored in a white background. It's organic. Girls will love it."

"It can be fun for parties, too!" Horace chimed in. The group was feverish with side-talk considering the idea.

Fredericka spoke again and everyone was at attention. "I have over thirty individual salt types, different notes, all colors, and flavors. With all the chilies, herbs, and vegetables we have close at hand, not to mention all the wine from the California glut, it's not expensive to make."

"Well, Fredericka, I'd like to see some numbers on that. Ever done a business plan?"

"I'll bring it next week," she told Bert as she sat down. "By the way, I also have a line of bar salts for drinks such as margaritas."

I took a chance and butted in. "Fredericka, would you like to display your *SeeSalts* right here? I have room in the retail area. I'd love to sell it here at the coffee shop."

"Love to," she said. "And here's a packet of the fresh citrus salt for you to try."

"Thanks," I said as I stowed it in my pocket, happy at the little gift that would be a treat at a future cocktail hour.

As the small plates emptied, I noticed that fingers and bread crusts were wiping every plate clean. The group was fortified and energetic about the idea and flavors enhanced by Fredericka's samples. She was flushed and giddy at her newfound attention.

"Neil, are you next?" asked Bert.

"Yes, everyone. I've come up with a devise to signal when you need to do a "U" turn. Cars signal right or left, but how about the unrepresented and often unnoticed "U" turn? It can be installed on shopping carts, baby strollers, bikes, and boats…"

On and on they went around the table, labor saving devices, green environment plans, and gadgets of all kinds.

Norman took a turn. "My idea is to help the world's over-population with supplying countries with condoms imprinted with baroque holy pictures. The instructions would state, not for the prevention of pregnancy, but for the prevention of communicable diseases." His presentation was met with booing and Bert took over again. "Let's just table that and move on. Who's next?"

Gordon shook the cuff of my sleeve, "Resa, do we have any birch sugar?"

"No, why?" It was back to my real time job.

"There's someone here who is insisting she only uses birch sugar. What should I tell her?" he asked worriedly.

"I'll talk to her…where is she?"

"Register, yellow shirt." Relieved, he hurried back to the assembly line behind the counter. My brief exposure to some Sedona natives was over but they would be back next week. Now, I was quizzing my mind's inventory on the existence of birch sugar. There wasn't another quiet minute the rest of that day after the Brainstormers left. The birch sugar patron delivered a lecture on the virtues of this ultra expensive alternative, complete with the dire warnings of white or raw sugar. She promised to bring her own supply along next time she stopped in for tea and lunch.

As the mid-morning progressed, I was grateful Lacey was spending her free day from spa treatments to help out in the coffee shop because a herd of tourists came galloping in. While she dispensed treatments such as the Symphony Massage, the Malaysian Oil Stone Treatment or the Spanish Rosemary Body Scrub at her other job, I drooled. If I could ever get a two-hour break, I wanted to get one of the treatments I heard her describe. I was a poster child for spa therapy.

By eleven in the morning, the dining room and patio were jam-packed and we raced to keep up. The café was an assembly-line of lunches and drinks. We were jammed, slammed, and damned. I was dishing up salads; garnishes were flying. Barry manned the register and Gordon and Gerry were in top form. The customers kept Lacey and Grant running until well past 4:00 pm. The last few hours brought in thirsty customers looking for a boost, a snack or something sweet as a tea-time treat. Barry eyeballed me and sidled up next to my arm.

"My little Resa Peanut Butter Cup, this is going to be our biggest day ever, a record breaker." He was pleased. "We'll go over a thousand in sales by six," he said.

"If we did that everyday, we could pay ourselves a salary," I groused. "Let's start the clean-up early, my Potato Latke," I advised.

"I couldn't work this hard everyday," Barry answered.

Barry liked the calmer flow of life, never pushing too hard. He needed to laugh, mock, or chill everyday and had made mention of the fact that his family ostracized him for sidelining his degrees in higher education. They had strong expectations of Barry using his credentials. He was the family's rebel, the white sheep.

It took us two hours to clean up and reload for the anticipated Sunday morning crowd. They were the group that never sleeps in, as well as the East Coast contingency whose biological clock was set three hours earlier. Sunday services were out of the question for me, just not enough time, but I missed the ritual and music. The Lutheran church was on my way to the coffee shop and I hoped a drive-by would suffice. Sedona's spiritualism and sayings replaced the hymnal. So the harder we worked on any given day, the more tail work we had. By the time I got home, I realized I was famished, exhausted, and dehydrated, even too tired to pet my ever expectant and faithful dog, Skye. Barry trailed in behind me. He was tired and bark-less. He offered to mix a carafe of margaritas.

"Get me a glass of cold water first," I begged, kicking off my shoes and pulling at a food-splattered apron. "Otherwise, I'll get looped."

"Hope so," Barry replied. The blender was already buzzing.

"I have a cache of Fredericka's lime salt to add to cocktail time," I said.

As we licked the salt-rimmed glasses, inhaling the fresh lime scent, we armchair quarterbacked the day. Grant had completely forgotten an order for a guy at a table for four. That cost us a $15.00 free lunch and an apology. Gerry had been caught talking on his cell phone four times while customers bore down. Katy, the new golden girl, kept fingering the jewelry on the necks of the female clients talking stones and minerals while the line grew longer and longer. Six pieces of silverware were found in the trash. The floor mops were left soaking in stinky, dirty water instead of being rinsed, disinfected, and hung out to dry. The men's room cleaning was missed and grimy all day. All in all a typical day, but our first, full-flush day.

While Barry whipped up a second round, I had a thick filet of halibut oiled and herbed with thyme and broiling in a hot oven. As it meandered into semi-doneness, a quick field-green salad was washed, spun dry and assembled in ninety seconds tops. Then two gray Mexican lita squash were cubed and micro-waved into a mildly steamed second course. Before he could take stock of my movements, I flipped a piece of puff pastry over the half-cooked fish and lowered the oven temperature. As I limped back to the couch to resume our dissection of the day's activities and enjoy another citrus-flavored drink, I asked Barry to put out two plates and silverware.

We were relaxing, being uplifted on the tequila and the aromas from the kitchen. "I didn't even know how hungry I was," he said.

"Yeah, we'll have dinner in fifteen more minutes, mentally calculating the time the puff pastry would need to finish. "Dinner will be ready when the timer goes off."

"How'd you make something so fast? Where'd you get the energy?"

"Don't know. Somehow it just happened," I replied.

"Resa, we can't keep working at this pace," he began. "You know, I see you taking care of everything, of everyone, worrying all the time...you've done it all your life. Who worries about you?"

"Right now, I think you're using some of your old psychology degree on me!" I just wanted to enjoy dinner so I could stretch out, relax, and get in the hot tub. I wasn't ready to think about a caretaker for me or the absence of one. I avoided answering any more of the questions hanging in the air now surrounded by the scrumptious dinner aromas.

Barry came over to where I was stretched out on the couch and slowly pulled the ottoman close by. Very carefully, he picked up my work-weary, right hand in between both of his and ever so gently began to press and massage it in between both of his. It was the hand that had multiple splits on the thumb and fingers. A painful boney lump had been growing larger on the back of my hand.

"I mean it, Resa. We can't go on like this and I can't stand seeing you so tired. I'm worried something's going to happen to you."

I turned my head into the couch cushions so Barry couldn't see the tears that were starting to creep into my eyes. No one had ever held my hand like that and spoken so empathetically. Instead of answering, I took back my weary paw, sliding it from beneath his concern and hopped up as the oven timer announced, "Dinner!"

Chapter 17

THE CALENDAR TOLD ME that today was my birthday… usually a day to pamper myself a little, plan a small party with my son and daughters and have a dinner out, but not this year. I was relaxing for a few delightful minutes while engrossed in the memory of how nice a reclining position felt. Due to some advanced planning, I had the fresh specials for the coffee shop prepped ahead of time. More than anything, my birthday gift to myself this year was going to be a couple of hours wrapped in a flannel blanket, couched with a good novel, and eight heavenly hours of deep sleep to follow. The girls at the clinic had put on a buffet lunch as a way to acknowledge my "*bonn anniversaire.*" I was just putting my feet up and letting my mind slide backwards to review my day. I had had a 'no repeat day.' All my films had been on target; something every X-ray tech wants every workday. Usually one or two repeats were acceptable but a hundred-percent day was sweet! Just as I was about to start my quiet evening, the phone rang.

"Get dressed," Barry announced. "We're going to go out for a birthday cocktail."

"Oh, that's sweet," I said. "But I'll pass."

"I'm on my way," Barry replied.

"Good grief, no," I protested. "Let's just have a quick toast here. Early morning tomorrow, you know."

"I'm on your doorstep. We're going out. The evening is waiting M'Lady." Then the doorbell rang. I was a rabbit in a hole. There was no choice but to answer the door and let him in.

"Wow," was my comment as I looked over his spruced-up look, a total transformation. He was dressed in his best: pressed oxford shirt, tie, slacks, and sport coat. He rocked back on his heels smiling in his 'sexy-try-me-out-smile' letting my eyes glide up and down, welcoming my scrutiny. He was easy that way — on occasion, a flashy dresser.

So I put on something from the back of the closet, something never worn before and sheer; after all, it was my birthday. Barry was already pacing the floor, talking to himself and polishing his Don Rickles' lines from an ancient tape.

"So, *I say to you, you can't live in my neighborhood*"... his borrowed lines were new again and I found myself

149

laughing at his performance that echoed through the rooms. He was pacing as he joked, holding the cigar he never smoked as an invisible microphone. He carried it as an accessory to add to his glammed-up-look.

"Ah, Barry, I'm ready." He answered with a wolf whistle.

As we drove towards town it was not possible to overlook the fading shadows on the cliffs at dusk. The sunset was another spectacular production nature devised to keep us humble and I somehow wanted to capture that magnificent pinkish-gold cloud color that was a showstopper. My mind turned to creating a new dish and in an instant a vision of mashed sweet potatoes with a puddle of prickly pear syrup, the color of the evening sky came to me. They would be called *Ocoso Arcendia* or sunset potatoes in Spanish.

"We need to stop at the café for a few minutes," Barry said, as he wheeled his car right into the closest parking spot by the darkened store. When he ordered me to follow him in, I didn't protest. As he unlocked the door and allowed me to pass in front of him, I heard the scurrying sounds that mice can make and I blinked at the now empty dining room, empty except for just one lone table, set with linens, lighted candles, tabletop ware, wine glasses, and flowers.

"Where are all the tables? The café is empty," I gasped.

"Just be patient," Barry answered.

From behind the counter four familiar faces were lined up watching my surprise, eyes shining, smiles back at mine. The sound system had a lovely purr of Etta James's old tune, *At Last*, filtering through and some ambrosial smells were coming from the kitchen. Along with their mother, Mrs. Greenly, the boys rang out in unison a Tagalog accented, "Happy Birthday, Resa!"

It was sweet and I was impressed, but they weren't done. They stood in line and each one presented a gift: Gordon, a clear, quartz crystal and an offer for a free tattoo; Gerry, a bottle of green oil balanced to my zodiac sign; Grant, a box of incense. Mama Greenly had prepared a dinner from her own special repertoire of favorites; it consisted of black, mustard-seeded rice, a chicken adobo and a cold ginger, cucumber salad. Barry was popping a split of *Moet* and *Chandon* Champagne as the four scurried out the door, leaving us in the darkened spacious room alone.

"This, dear Resa, is just for you and called, 'Table for Two.' Happy Birthday!" Barry announced.

As I turned to him with the appreciation for all his effort and secret plans, Barry caught my wrist and in an instant, a gold bangle slipped over my hand. Taking me into his arms, he pulled me close. We stepped into the music and danced and danced and danced.

Chapter 18

BOBBY BEGAY WAS UP to his old tricks. He only had to look in the mirror each morning to know he was handsome, handsomer than his dad, who had played the role of a Native American many times in the westerns filmed in Sedona in the 1940's. He sat across from his friend, Flint Painted Horse, at their favorite table at the Weathervane, in the far corner, backs to the wall, surveying the room. They were waiting for Dakota, Flint's younger sister who was always late.

'When did she say she'd be here?" he asked.

She didn't.

"Dakota time."

"Yeah, but when she walks in, watch all the old geezers."

"Yeah, ha, ha."

Bobby stuck his feet out when he saw me coming with the refill coffee pot. His long legs of faded denim stretched for miles. Playing a child's game, he dared me to cross; he held me with his eyes, the stare of a wolf. That look was pure sweet talk that made me wonder what it would be like, Navaho style.

He wasn't about to pull the long appendages in and indicated by a nod of his head that I should step over. So I turned and headed out to the patio, a steaming pot of freshly brewed Colombian in hand. Refills were needed by the Intergalactic Space Travelers who shared stories of space alien abductions and visitations from extra-terrestrial beings. One member of their group busily knitted with huge needles.

"What are you working on?" I asked as I refreshed the cups.

Shilo answered, "A crop circle rug, you know, with the design of a well-known crop circle that *they* left as a message."

As I came back into the coffee shop, I couldn't help but sneak another look in Bobby's direction. He was one gorgeous example of manhood.

His lusty looks and how much time Bobby loafed around the coffee shop told me one thing since his arrivals coincided with my schedule: I was being watched. My dreams kept me busy with imaginary scenes of love *a la* Native American-style starring the very sexy, Bobby Begay.

In spite of the longing looks from Bobby, or maybe because of them, I added him and Flint Painted Horse and their cousin, Dakota, to the invitees for the first Thanksgiving dinner at the Café. There would be a potluck for the side dishes and I would prepare the turkey grilled "Sedona Ranch" style. I gave Gordon the task of a hatchet job on two fourteen-pound turkeys. After much swagger and showing off of knife sharpening, he cut the fowl into generous serving pieces.

A dry-rub coated and flavored the bird with medium hot red chili, garlic and manzanita, and other secret ingredients. A mesquite-smoked salt added in the last quarter hour of baking on hot cast iron plates in the oven would impart a crisp skin and an outdoor grilled aroma.

Added to the banquet was a tureen of a mélange of pureed carrot, parsnip, and turnip. The other side dishes included creamed spinach, mashed buttermilk potatoes, fresh sage bread stuffing, yeasty rolls, gravy, a cranberry-prickly pear relish, and a cranberry-apple wine.

My family played the part of the proverbial Pilgrims, and the Native Americans were in attendance as Bobby Begay and Flint Painted Horse and Dakota had accepted as soon as I mentioned the feast. In honor of their attendance, I had prepared one of Flint's favorites; a stuffed acorn squash baked with a filling of leek-seasoned, wild rice and chopped buffalo meat. The fragrance in the coffee shop was intoxicating with good cheer and an expectation of the feast to come.

On one side of the room, giggles and small talk

enveloped Lacey and Jimmy who had been progressing towards partnership by discussing the all-important questions of their future, while in another corner Grandma walked in octogenarian circles carrying an empty plate and purposefully asking over and over, "What should I do next?". The party went on till midnight.

Outside the sky grew cloudy and suggested a drizzle. The wind began to rattle the windows and sent the coppery scent of red rock dust under the doorsill.

Chapter 19

IN MARCH, USUALLY THE busiest time of the year in Sedona, there was news, rumors, and activity at the Dry Creek Plaza. We would be gaining some neighbors. Tenants were signing on and beginning to move into the building. The shelled-out spaces were being rented and plans were being made. The beautiful building had been brought to life; it was alive again with my Weathervane Café and now others saw the virtues of the location.

Trenches were dug in the parking lot and cornered off with yellow tape. We knew not why. Deliveries were arriving. Often the truckers came into the coffee shop first, looking for someone whose name we did not recognize, someone to accept and sign for a load of material.

Our first new neighbor arrived with no disturbances

156

or problems. Within a week an empty space behind the coffee shop became a calming retreat; a bookstore complete with the old library smells associated with volumes, ink and paper. Not only was the owner, Pete, a nice guy, he shared plans for workshops, later hours and business expanding ideas. He soon got addicted to our chicken wrap and chocolate chip cookies. His group discussion meetings and writers' workshops would require a river of coffee.

He didn't have any further information about the open trenches in the parking lot, but let us know an "institute" would be built out in the largest space in the building's lower level. A few professionals such as an accountant and a marriage counselor were moving in upstairs, he shared.

Pete and Barry kibitzed for a few minutes each day, exchanging gossip, sipping scalding coffee, and testing the morning's pastries.

"I recommended that Ranjit give the bookstore some help," Barry told me.

"Oh?"

"Seems like Ranjit needs some outside jobs; they're not making enough money with the bakery even though Dipti is baking morning, noon, and night. Ranjit is doing all the deliveries and says he needs to get away as much as he can...I'm worried about those two."

"Why?" I asked, wrapping up my assortment of herbed butters.

"They're changing every time they come in here," he related.

"How so?"

"No more robes, just average clothes…they're not happy. I caught them arguing out in the parking lot and Dipti, I mean Betty, was smoking a cigarette…"

"Really, there's trouble in Nirvana? Next they'll be eating meat, drinking liquor, and dancing," I projected.

"I'm going to call the landlord and find out when those trenches will be filled. It's hurting business, looks bad, and goofy Grant tripped the other day."

"Barry, I need to leave a half hour earlier today. Doctor's appointment," I confessed.

"What's wrong?" he asked.

"My thumb's triggering from too much work. I've got to get it looked at," I admitted. "So, Pete has no idea what the mysterious institute will be?"

"No one seems to know. There are workmen over there, but no main honcho or owner. No one's talking. I'll see what I can squeeze out of Stein. The workmen are in here everyday for lunch. Business is up," he said.

"I can tell by how much more I'm cooking…and by how sore this is," I whined, holding up an aching thumb with bandages on the fingertips.

Local rumors around town informed me that Bernard Stein never wanted that ark of a building in Sedona. It was his wife, Charlotte Stein, who just had to have it, to add to her ever-burgeoning portfolio: the Trust. She was blonde, beautiful, and rich. And her contributions to the community bode well for her husband's real estate office.

The lovely Charlotte was thrilled about our intentions

even though Barry and I presented as a mismatched couple. She told Stein we sounded credible and our plans could only help erase the dingy sandwich shop, turning it into a charming tearoom or coffee shop. Stein never thought we were solid, even though, as the manager, Barry was a Lanceman, a mensch. Stein never wanted us in the building, but he did it to get "Her Gorgeousness" off his neck and keep the write-offs clean.

Moonbeam announced Barry's call to Stein. Our old building had been vacant for years: complete with problems in the wiring, plumbing, air-conditioning, and landscaping as well as a leaking roof. Stein was plagued by taxes and the rising insurance premiums. Tenants always wanted blood, but tenants meant rent.

When Barry called, the long interlude "on hold" gave the message: *Not them again.*

"Yes, Barry?" There was no, "How can I help you?" Stein was never one to agree to anything the lease hadn't spelled out.

Barry did his best to pull out information on the trenches, the air-conditioners failing to cool, and "who" the new mysterious neighbors would be. He came away with less information than his talk with Bookstore Pete.

"By the way, Stein," added Barry, "about the open trenches, one of the employees and a little old lady slipped yesterday and almost fell in."

Chapter 20

THERE WERE A DOZEN new bottles in the glass fronted beverage cooler. The flowers on the label caught my eye as I went past. This was new; I'd never seen this product in the coffee shop before.

"So what's this stuff?" I had a bottle of the clear liquid in hand. I was quizzing Gordon as Barry was nowhere to be found. The label told me it was "vibrationally infused" with the essence of the energy of different flowers: lilies, roses, and marigolds. I read on, not understanding the process and as I cracked the cap and took a swig, I expected to taste something perfumed, rosy, and fragrant. Water was what I tasted: cool, clean, pure nothing.

Gordon just shrugged. His English was improving and everyone had learned his morning greeting of *Mabuhay*, pronounced ma-boo-high, which means hello, welcome, or greetings.

I found Barry rearranging the heavy number-ten cans in the large pantry that we used for storage. It was an under-the-staircase closet now holding a supply of dry goods.

"What gives?" I asked, holding up a bottle of water with a pretty floral label. "No taste…"

"It's not supposed to have a taste," he mumbled. He wasn't in the mood to talk in the cramped hot quarters as he hoisted heavy boxes and case lots.

"Not supposed to have a taste?" my voice edged up a little higher in disbelief. I was stuck on taste. This coffee shop was all about taste and flavor.

"The energy is instilled into the water from the flowers. That is what the guy said." He wanted to get rid of my questions and me.

"Okay, start from the beginning. What guy, what energy, where?"

Barry gave up rotating the canned goods and came out of the tightly packed storeroom. His backhand swipe wiped some sweat from his forehead. He took the bottle from my hand and took a long drink.

"See, there's no taste," I pointed that out again.

"So, this guy comes in a few days ago with a case of these energetically instilled flower waters and talks me into trying them. He tells me, 'Just try twenty-four and see how they sell.' It's supposed to be popular all over town." He swigged another long drink.

"I just don't get it," I said. "How do you get a flower's vibration into water?"

"I don't know."

"I can't believe you fell for this one, Barry. I thought you were smarter than that. These will never sell, not at this price! The price is triple for the same number of ounces of plain bottled water." In a fury, I stomped off after grabbing the Anasazi beans. I needed to cook up something Native American style, adding Barry's scalp for flavor. As I passed the life-sized cardboard image of Dipti, I noticed she now sported some blackened teeth, little devil horns above her forehead, and a thin mustache.

On my way back to the prep area, I overheard Gordon giving his brothers a history lesson.

"Alright then, who is the queen of England?" asked Gordon.

"Elton John," answered Gerry.

"That's correct. But who is the old queen?"

"Dame Edna?" answered Grant in an unsure voice.

"Let's try something easier," continued Gordon, now rising from his chair. "If the President is killed, who runs the United States?"

Grant waved his hand furiously like a schoolboy vying for the teacher's attention. Gordon nodded to him.

"The First Lady," Grant answered.

"That's correct."

"Now, what are the last words of the National Anthem of the United States?"

"Play ball!" yelled out Gerry.

"Once again, correct," said Gordon proudly.

People in the coffee shop were watching, listening in and laughing quietly to themselves. I stepped out from behind the counter to see Barry watching intently with a broad smile.

"Barry, this is ridiculous," I whispered.

"I know, but it's just too much fun to watch. Listen in, it'll get better. I know it will," said Barry.

Gordon was now pacing back and forth in front of his two students. "Now who runs the military of the United States?"

The guesses from Gerry and Grant came swiftly, "Captain Crunch, Colonel Klink, and General Foods?"

"One of you didn't study for this," said Gordon in a slow, warning voice. "Very well then, what are the four branches of the military?"

A moment of awkward silence finally ended as Grant raised an unsure hand. Gordon nodded.

Grant spoke slowly and without confidence. "I can name three, "The Salvation Army, Old Navy, and Air Force One."

"You forgot the Right Guard, Gordon, they have aerosol weapons," piped in Gerry.

Gordon announced, "We must return to work. More higher education tomorrow."

I looked at Barry, who simply smiled and shook his head in disbelief.

While I was sizzling the onions, carrots, and pieces of juicy lamb, Ned tapped me on the shoulder. The Anasazi beans were ready to become an authentic tribal dish. If the tourist didn't understand the origin of the bean and savor the regional flavors, the locals would. The pungent smells of wild marjoram and simmering lamb perked everyone's mood in the café. It was short-lived, however, when Ned stepped away from the middle-aged female customer to rasp a question in my ear, as I dreamily stirred the bean soup.

"That lady wants to know about the salad dressing." He turned to look back towards the gray-haired biddy at the register, now looking straight at me. "No kitchen" also meant a lack of privacy. My cooking was always on display.

"What do you mean?" I groped for more information, putting down my spoon, wiping my hands on my apron, and ready to put out another fire.

"She just ordered a Zuni Spinach Salad and is asking about the dressing."

Our Prickly Pear Salad Dressing was unprecedented, fantastic, and captured the extraordinary flavor of the one unshared flavor note of the fruit of the cactus. It was singular among flavors; the flavor a delightful plum-cranberry essence, unlike any other taste on Earth. Gathered in the fall, these thorny orbs have a tart, thick wall of fruit. The black rounded seeds are webbed in a spongy juicy net. The fruit is magenta and stains your hands as it is blanched, skinned, seeded, and turned into a useable product. Health benefits abound from the flavoinoids. Sweetened, it tastes heavenly, and as I opened my gallon jars shipped from Cheri's in Tucson, I inhaled the fragrant bouquet deeply and allowed myself several spoonfuls of the fresh delicious jelly. We carried both the jelly and syrup, using the jelly to sweeten the salad dressing and the kiddies' peanut butter and jelly sandwiches. The syrup flavored the pink lemonade.

I would daydream about a long walk to gather the nopales to cook up a batch of fresh prickly pear jelly. In the late fall, when the prickly pears were a deep magenta color, they could be harvested and processed. I would take a five-gallon pail, leather gloves, a sharp knife, and a pair of long handled tongs as I set out on a hike. As I sliced the ripe fruit from the pads, I was careful to keep the thorny spines away from my skin.

Back at home, I scorched the thorns off each pear as I held it by the tongs over a gas flame. Now de-thorned, each one was dropped in ice water to blanch. Next came the easy peeling and a quick scooping out of the center seedpod. What remained was a wall of fleshy fruit now ready for sauces, sorbet, jelly, or candy.

Now I approached the customer with a question on her face. She had a dish of the Zuni Spinach Salad in her hand. After a ritual smile, introduction, and offer of help, I got to the bottom of her concerns. It took a series of questions and answers. It was the sugar problem again!

"Yes," I answered, "the salad dressing is sweetened with a jelly from the fruit of the cactus. So, can I offer you another dressing, such as our Cilantro Lime, with no sugar, ma'am?"

"No, thanks, I keep a bottle of my salad dressing in my car. I'll be right back," she said, finalizing the sale.

I just shook my head in disbelief.

◆◆◆◆◆◆◆◆◆◆

"There's a problem you're gonna have to take care of, Resa," complained Barry.

"What's that?" I asked, kneeling to add the information about the Anasazi Bean Soup to the large blackboard on the wooden easel.

"It's time to fire Grant. He's just too undependable," Barry said. "You have to do it."

"Why me? What's he done now? You're the manager."

"Yeah, but you're the owner. And this job is his whole world. He's late every day, eats his allowed meal as soon as he gets here, and, well, there's been a lot of things I haven't told you."

"What things?" We had now stepped out to the patio.

"Yesterday he closed the store two hours early and told Katy to go home."

"Yesterday?" I repeated.

"Yeah, you were at the clinic and I ran up to Flagstaff to pick up the goods we ordered. Besides that, the final straw, he came in on the wrong day. Sometimes he comes in on the wrong shift, too."

I was shaking my head. Of the three brothers, Grant was the sweetest and most demonstrably affectionate. He told me frequently that he "loved me" in a puppyish way

166

and that he loved the coffee shop and his job.

"The other day he took it upon himself to turn a single café mocha for Joel, the owner of the health food store, into two half cups. He served one to Joel's girlfriend. She doesn't even drink coffee and the mood was lost for Joel by the time I fixed it."

"Oh, no," I gasped.

"Then the other day he made up a to-go order, put the china plate under the sandwich and into the styrofoam box and sent it out. Customer brought the plate back later and complained."

"My eyebrows were up. "Oh, I see," I murmured.

"Resa, you have to do it!" Barry had backed me into a corner.

Oh, by the way, why did you talk to Roland so long today? Problems?" Barry asked.

"No, no problems. There's an upcoming trade show in Phoenix at the Civic Center. All the purveyors will be there. We were just discussing some culinary things," I answered.

"Like what?"

"Like white truffle soup, a good *Chevalier-Montrachet*, a taste of unsalted sturgeon caviar…"

"Out of my league, my little Sugar Cookie," he said, as he headed back to work. "And by the way, that case of flower water is gone. It sold like crazy!"

◆◆◆◆◆◆◆◆◆◆

The coffee beans go up for bid on the Hong Kong futures market, the Hang Sang, five times a day starting at 9:30 AM. The big names jump on the futures in the first round, covering their demands for the next week. Their buyers backed off the next three sessions, letting the little guys squabble over the bean prices at 10:30 AM, 1:30 PM and 2:30 PM. The Arabica is bid on before the Robusta is presented.

The heavy hitters get their calls in for the last session, picking off the last scraps and cleaning up any bean left behind. The market price could swing as much as forty cents between sessions, wiping out the small players. Ron Everett, our coffee rep, left a message to expect that our coffee prices would be going up again.

Chapter 21

/ / So what did the doctor say?" Barry asked.

We were having a juicy burger at the Biker Bar atop Cleopatra Hill in Jerome. Since Lacey and Jim had never seen the copper mining town, once known as the "wickedest" town in the west, they tagged along. The panoramic vista gave a view that ran fifty miles from a high perch on the edge of the mountain.

"Can't have any more injections after this. Surgery is the next option," I said between bites, waving my bandaged thumb. It was taped with a splint and was painful.

The beer was draught and ice cold, just the way I liked it. Lacey and Jimmy were shooting some pool.

"I think this new girl, Katy, is going to be able to help out. She has no other commitments and says she knows about food," Barry advised.

"I'm not sure about her yet, Bar," I replied.

"Why's that?" he asked, ready to defend his new hire.

"Well, she told me some strange things about herself. I'm still giving her time. We'll see, that's all," I said.

"What are you keeping from me?"

"Let's just see, okay?" I said.

"Hey, looks like those two are quite a pair," Barry said, motioning toward Lacy and Jimmy.

"Maybe, my future son-in-law," I whispered.

"So you know something about Katy you're not telling?" Barry asked.

"Let's just say she's had a very difficult childhood," I said.

Later, as we descended on the switchback curves to the valley below and made our way back to the coffee shop, I made a mental note to be on the alert for trouble ahead.

♦♦♦♦♦♦♦♦♦♦

The bakery that Ranjit, formerly George, had designed for his illuminated partner in love, Dipti, was compact. It was a miracle in efficiency. Ranjit had a knack for the mechanical and applied it to save space, everything a step or less away from Dipti's fingertips. He had even devised a custom slicing system to precisely divide the baked goods, sans sugar, into perfectly edged serving pieces. His wrapping technique made the carrot cake, applesauce spice, and zucchini cakes look highly professional.

Since Ranjit had personally expanded their client list, Dipti couldn't keep up; she was baking for hours on-end once she cranked up the *Viking* oven. She hadn't been out of the bakery since Monday night; she hadn't been out of the house for a week.

At night, Ranjit un-wrapped the plastic from the unsold four-day-old cakes he brought back from the route. Enjoying the Sedona evening as the temperatures cooled down, he sat on his back porch alone and tossed the stale sweets into the arroyo. He needed some time to regroup after the latest brew-ha-ha with Dipti, the fights and arguments that came from her being overwhelmed.

◆◆◆◆◆◆◆◆◆◆

Katy, our golden girl, was now in her fourth week of work at the coffee shop. By all outward appearances, she was going to be the fastest trainee that Barry hired. She understood cleanliness, using wet and dry cloths always at hand. Her skill at prepping the raw vegetables for the daily salads was above average and instructions and suggestions were absorbed at first mention.

I had a few sayings I used with the three brothers. The first was, "Clean, clean, clean" and the second was, "Brown is bad, except for UPS." As a healthcare worker, I prided myself on my compulsive cleanliness at the coffee shop. There was a constant struggle to keep the guys as fastidious as I required.

"So what's wrong between Katy and Ned?" I asked an

aside to Barry.

"He doesn't like her," he answered.

"Know why?"

"Ned doesn't like anyone, but he says she's lazy and has everyone fooled, mostly you."

It was my job to keep an eye on this interaction. I was hoping for some smooth sailing on the turbulent seas of the ever-changing employee tide. Alerted to Barry's observation that there was some negative interaction between Katy and Ned, I arrived a little early on a Tuesday to get a little paperwork done before starting my shift. Katy had manned the floor while Ned was behind the register.

I slipped in behind the counter and grabbed a quick coffee, completely unnoticed by either employee. I took a seat at a corner table and quietly sipped my drink with my head down as I poured over my work. After a few minutes, I left the coffee shop for my upstairs office where I had a view of the whole room from an open casement window in the hallway.

"Katy, watch the register for me. I've got to take care of some kitchen work," yelled Ned from across the room. He didn't wait to get an answer. He simply left.

Katy was pretty busy but managed both jobs fairly well. I peaked from my portal above to see something disturbing. Ned wasn't doing much of anything. He was standing against a wall, watching Katy do both their jobs. I wanted to see what was up so I continued to silently watch.

A full five minutes passed. Finally Ned filled a sugar dispenser with salt, put it in his pocket and walked out front where Katy was totally swamped.

"Okay folks, okay, I'm here now. No need to panic," he announced. "Katy, you can go back to your tables. I'll handle this."

He was completely demeaning to her and tried to set himself up as if he were saving her from some situation she couldn't handle. The minute she looked away, he excused himself from the counter and switched the sugar dispensers with one on a nearby table. I continued to watch as a customer ruined an excellent mocha cappuccino with salt. Upon seeing the situation, he walked over and tasted the coffee.

"Oh my God, Katy. What did you do?" he said, loud enough for everyone to hear.

"Don't worry folks, I'll take care of this," he said, walking back behind the counter. He started to make a new coffee to replace the ruined one.

Katy didn't know what was going on except that she'd been embarrassed again. The poor girl stood red-faced and awkward, bussing a table and pretending not to care. I couldn't believe what I just saw. Ned was deliberately sabotaging the coffee shop to try to discredit a co-worker. Did he actually think he'd impress anyone by making someone else look incompetent?

I didn't have a replacement for him or I'd probably have fired him on the spot. Instead, I would make sure he and Katy worked separate shifts until I could replace him or have a serious talk with him.

I cleared my throat and walked down to the front counter and picked up the salt loaded sugar dispenser. Ned looked at me as if he were about to pass a kidney stone. Setting my empty cup in front of him, I asked, "What's wrong Ned? You look like you're stressed out." I took the sugar dispenser and poured the salt down the prep sink drain while my eyes locked onto his. He was caught for possibly the first time in his life. "You know, I read guilt can bring on serious stress. Yes, that's what the article said. Guilt was the cause."

I then turned my attention to Katy. "Ned's going to stay late and help me with my shift. That's okay with you Ned, right?"

"Oh sure," he answered.

"Katy, since I've got the extra help, why don't you take a half-hour break. That's okay with you, isn't it Ned?" I asked.

"Yeah, sure. I didn't see you come in. How long were you here?" he asked.

I didn't say a word. He didn't deserve an answer. I'd just let him worry about it.

Chapter 22

THE INCOME STREAM AT the Weathervane Café fluctuated with the tourist season. It was heavy in March, April, and October, averaging out in between with the lows in August and September: the hot months. Sales needed to be twenty to fifty percent higher or this would always be a non-profit business and the line of credit now at a whooping $50K would still be owed to the bank at the end of the lease. My only recourse was to increase hours, add a liquor license, and make dinner available at least on the weekends. Many of Sedona's full-time residents never found the coffee shop; they were the crowd who came out for a special dinner in their town. They weren't looking for a workingman's lunch or a tourist stop. As I formulated plans for tasty pizzas in the afternoons, a distinctive dinner menu, and an opportunity for wedding parties to hold teas and rehearsal dinners, Barry stalled and resisted. Rent per day was the same whether we were open twelve or twenty hours a day.

I bought advertising and had a video commercial produced. Fancy teapots were acquired. I contacted the wedding guide in Sedona to let them know the café offered a Bridesmaids' Tea. Pizza sauce, good mozzarella cheese and raw basil were added to the weekly order, however no gourmet pizza materialized. Barry didn't want the extra hours, a bigger staff, and the responsibility of the coffee shop becoming a full service café. He especially did not want to see the Weathervane Cafe add beer and wine to the menu. For he would have the headaches that alcohol on the premises would bring: a lockable storage area for alcohol, additional recordkeeping, and surprise inspections from the Liquor Control Board.

Even as I was pushing for more productivity from the coffee shop, I was feeling more and more stressed and started experiencing elevated blood pressure and occasional chest pains. I cut down on the caffeine and missed the full-flavored brew each morning. A search was made for a tasty decaf to no avail and I missed my delicious morning coffee. A sound night's sleep was rare with all the worries.

Barry and I were discussing the brass ring of more income. To be honest, I was talking expansion of services and Barry was playing opossum. We rarely argued in the past but the subject of the proposed changes created several rounds of white-hot nuclear exchanges.

"All right, so tell me, Barry, exactly why aren't you in favor of longer hours?" I asked.

"I'm already doing enough. I work enough. I work as much as I wanna work."

"Wait a minute... That wasn't our deal, Barry."

"Well, what's the deal? That's the way I remember it, my Scrumptious Crumpet."

"Don't scrumptious crumpet me, you keg of goose fat," I countered as my temper flared. "You've got a copy of the deal in your files. Go read it again!"

"All I know is that this business has changed both of us and is starting to kill you," he retorted.

"What I am saying ... after the figures that Sterling presented me, and what you've been telling me, is that even at the end of the three year lease at this rate, I'm still in debt fifty thousand dollars. Explain that one to me."

"Well, there aren't enough customers. Uh, I don't know but... I'm already doing all that I feel I'm able to do."

"Ha, ha. You know what? That's a joke! Because not only am I a woman and I'm ten years older than you, you punk, but you know what? I have two jobs. And I gave you this job and it's up to you to make this place work. Profitability. You've got to do it."

"Hey, watch it with the name calling. So, you think that's up to me?

"That's right.

"Well... I, I don't know what to do. Sedona is ...well maybe, maybe this is the wrong place."

"That's not the issue or the reality, Barry. Making more income with increased sales is the salvation, the only answer."

"Well, I, for one, am tired"

"You, for one, are on your second strike out."

"So let me hear what your glorious new expansion plans are, Ms. Forbes."

"For starters we need to have the young kids coming in here after school for pizzas. We need some of the parents, too."

"Pizzas are a pain in the ass."

"I don't care if they're a pain in the ass. People want the fresh raw basil, the good sauce..."

"Well, the kids aren't gonna buy that. They're gonna buy the cheap shit. They don't give a rat's ass about the good stuff."

"And we need to add some small plates and tapas because that's what everybody wants right now. And you have to get over this liquor thing. We must have the beer and wine license. I'm tired of waiting."

"Oh... tapas, fapas," he mocked.

"No, it's the third time I've sent the application for booze in. All of the errors are YOUR information."

"So, I mixed up the dates, big deal."

"What's that I hear? ... Barry, what's that I hear? Barry, the cops are here!"

"No, they're not. That's just a fire truck."

"No, I swear. I can see them right here." I was peeking around the doorway." Come on, we gotta straighten this out. A couple of cops are here."

"What? Aw, they just want coffee. Coffee and donuts... They're cops!"

We ended our red-hot debate in the sink room real fast. At first, I clammed up thinking our argument pulled in the police. There were only two patrons in the café, finishing their cheesecakes, sans cat hair. Officers Sanders and Taylor of Sedona's finest introduced themselves, giving Barry and I a breather from our private fracas.

Sanders was the one in charge. They were smartly uniformed, cool and to the point.

"Do you have an employee by the name of Gerry Greenly?" Sanders asked in an official manner.

I answered in the affirmative. Barry was hanging back instead of his usual front door act. Out of the corner of my eye I could see that Gerry was silently backing into the tight corner near the make table. He was not visible to the policemen.

"Was he here today, Ma'am?" Sanders asked. I took umbrage at the reference to "the Ma'am."

"Why do you want to know?" I replied, now feeling a little annoyed at these guys coming into my place of business.

"That's between the Police Department and Mr. Greenly," Sanders answered. Taylor was not making a peep. "We need to talk to him."

Gerry stepped forward and faced the cops. As soon as they saw him, they knew they had their man. They asked him to step outside on the patio for a few words.

Barry and I just stared as Gerry shuffled out, dragging his feet. He walked slowly from behind the counter and around front. The cops escorted him outside to the patio.

We watched as a conversation ensued. Luckily, no other customers were in sight as Gerry was talking rapidly with choppy English and big hand gestures. Both cops had him boxed in, and he was getting more and more agitated. We couldn't hear a thing; the glass doors were too thick. Just when I thought the drama was ending, a pair of handcuffs came out and Gerry was hooked up, hands behind his back.

Sanders popped back in and said, "Ma'am, he's going to the station to be booked and then to the County Jail. Just wanted to let you know."

I don't know what got into me. Maybe I was all hopped up from bickering with Barry over money, hours and more staff, but I flew from behind the counter and stood right in front of Sanders in a face-off.

"How dare you come in here to my business and interfere with my staff, my employee. He's just a boy, only twenty, how dare you?" What did he do?" I demanded.

Sanders just smiled and took his time. "He'll be at the station for an hour or so to be booked on charges, Ma'am."

"What charges?" I demanded again.

"That's not for me to disclose, Ma'am."

I was livid and now I could hear Gerry squealing, "I didn't do anything, Resa! I swear! I didn't do anything!" He had his face pressed up against the window; he was crying, his cheeks scarlet, blubbering over and over "I swear, I didn't do anything! Save me, Resa, save me!" as they dragged him away.

I was too mad to be in shock. I grabbed the phone and started punching numbers, false starts, stop, starts again. Jangled and rattled beyond clear thinking, I didn't know who to call or what to do.

I got Gordon on the line; he was in the middle of a big tattoo job and couldn't talk. Grant wasn't answering. A second call made to Gordon got me their mother's number. Tika Greenly answered on the second ring and I broke the bad news to her. We quickly agreed that Gerry was not going to jail if there was anything we could do about it: double mother power. The Greenly Family needed to act. The Law had just hauled off my fastest worker.

Barry brought a bit of levity to the panic. He used the other phone line to call the police station less than a quarter mile away to ask pertinent questions. Gerry could be bailed out for $1,200. After making Mama Greenly swear the family would take care of its own and I'd be paid back, I left Barry alone at the coffee shop and raced to the bank where my Christmas money waited. I got over to the police station before Gerry's ride to the County Jail. With the cash and a bit of paperwork an hour later I had my man back. The reason for the arrest was lost in a jumble of broken English, Tagalog, and tears.

◆◆◆◆◆◆◆◆◆◆

"Mom, you look like you could use the Raindrop

Therapy I learned today at the spa," Lacey said when she saw my slouched body and furrowed brows. "Come in tomorrow for a Bamboo Lemongrass Scrub," she tried again.

"Honey child, that sounds great, but it won't fix a thing."

Chapter 23

THERE WAS A MESSAGE on my phone later that week identifying the caller as Zelda, who heard through the Sedona gossip hotline that I could use some help. I found out as we shared a pot of white peony tea that she had extensive experience with her own food businesses and as a private chef. Zelda wouldn't drop names but let me know she had cooked for the visiting stars and was still a troubleshooter for Sedona's most elegant Mediterranean restaurant. She could be the answer to the longer hours I needed and for weekend dining. Zelda wanted to work on her terms; a fly-in and fly-out food angel.

This time I had an update for Barry, so I phoned him at home to share the news. Before I could tell him about the extra chef power, he dropped a bombshell.

"Katy's been telling customers her sad history. Seems she was born into a Satanic cult and blabs about it all day. When I got wind of it and asked her about it, she walked out." It was more employee drama and another position short.

"One more thing, we had a fire on the roof early this morning. Firemen were in and out, tromping around. The oil leaked out of the sprinkler heads, the crew cleaned that up, but it still smells like a rotten egg fried in crude."

"Fire—on the roof?" I asked incredulously. "Any damage?" I was all ears.

"Called up to Flagstaff to ask the landlord about the fire…" he took a breath.

"Yeah?" I waited.

"Stein got on the phone personally and denied there even was a fire"

"I can't believe it!"

"Well, the firemen came back for lunch and, of course, the fire was real. They even brought their paramedic buddies and your green chili pork posole is all gone. They all ordered it. Oh, and another thing, Resa," he was on a roll. "A woman came in after she had lunch today. I've seen her in a couple of times now. She wants to book a private dinner for a group of thirty-five in two weeks. You need to give me some price quotes. She wants all the same salads we serve during the week and one main dish and a dessert."

"Book her, we need the extra income. This is what I was hoping for, Barry, dinner parties!" Before I could tell him about Zelda, he replied, "Be careful what you wish for."

♦♦♦♦♦♦♦♦♦♦

Barry met with the thirty-five person dinner party woman. I only knew her by the name, "Queenie." I penned out her menu and priced it and left the arrangements to Barry. Zelda would give me a hand since I had to do a half-day at the medical clinic the morning of Queenie's dinner party.

I got to have another chat with Roland. He promised to order three-dozen of the finest chicken breasts available for Queenie's dinner party. Diamonds, he called them. They would be skin-on and boneless. Today he wore a divine neroli blossom cologne that was driving me to distraction. I kept mixing up my quantities as we ordered for the special event. I planned to stuff the breasts with a fresh dill and spinach ricotta and do massive quantities of our most popular salads: the Zuni spinach salad with prickly pear dressing and the jicama with cilantro-lime. As a side dish, I would do a sweet parsnip-carrot puree and end with Morgan's prickly pear cheesecakes drizzled with fresh pink prickly pear syrup. Cat hair free, of course! The hostess wished to serve wine for her party if we could lock the doors and advertise a private party was in progress. That was within the realms of legality.

As Roland left with my order in hand, I gazed at an original watercolor hanging on the wall that I had purchased in Paris a few years ago. It centered on a French waiter I had named, Henri. Whenever dinner conversation stalled in my home, I would encourage a roundtable game; each guest must add a twisted paragraph to Henri's tragic life. As I looked at my cherished artwork on the wall of my struggling coffee shop, I realized Roland looked exactly like Henri, the Waiter.

Chapter 24

THE WEEKLY DELIVERY OF supplies from Make-O included two passes to the Restaurant Trade Show in Phoenix being held at the downtown Civic Center Plaza with a note urging the owners of the Weathervane Café to attend to view all new products, services, and the latest in all the food lines and appliances. After shoving the tickets around my desk for two weeks, there were several reasons to run down the hill and take care of several pressing issues and take a quick look at the spectacle in the Exhibition Hall.

Since Tika had called and needed to press the $1200 back into my hand personally from Gerry's brush from the law, mailing the money to me would not do, nor release her from the obligation. She explained that the duty to repay the debt was called *utag na loob* and that would be keeping with proper tradition. She referred to my action in keeping Gerry out of jail as a well-known Filipino trait that means "helping others," and that the native sense of *bayanihan* was in me. Gerry had lost a check and some unscrupulous individual had signed and forged his name. He hadn't done anything to break the law and the matter was cleared up on his court date.

I saved the food show for my last stop, estimating that it would take an hour or so to walk the aisles. What I needed was to acquire additional tabletop ware to be able to serve the dinner menu that I planned. I was also searching for a source of farm-raised quail and brook trout, endorsing the Sedona Ranch cuisine. By my estimation, my errands would be finished and with the two-hour return drive; I'd be home in time for bed and the early shift at the medical clinic.

The Exhibition Hall at the Civic Center was a factory of activity, sights, and tantalizing aromas from the vendor's samples. As I wandered from booth to booth, I realized there was a huge world of products and services unknown to my repertoire, my small coffee shop, and me. The mood was festive, the samples toothsome and generous and my eyes were opening to new ideas. I found the dinnerware and wine glasses that I needed for the coffee shop expansion. Now I could add a small plate selection and an evening dinner menu. Since they were so reasonably priced, I added twenty-four oversized salad plates that were perfect for soups, pastas, or gourmet presentations.

By the time I'd viewed the displays of exotic wild mushrooms, extra fine baby vegetables, and specialty meats and game, the show was closing for the evening. I had stayed until the bitter end but felt as if the French edition of *Larousse Gastronomique* had been installed into my brain. As I turned a corner to head for the exit, a voice called out my name.

"Resa, hey there…"

I turned around to come face to face with Roland, whom I had never expected to see.

"Enjoy the show?" he asked.

"I can't tell you how much! Remarkable, it's immense." I was already flustered and flabbergasted.

"What did you like the best?" he asked.

"Oh, the new products, the gourmet items like the wild mushrooms and the choice meats on display. It will make adding on dinners easy with the availability." I was looking down into my bag of samples, brochures, and business cards.

"Did you see our display? Make-O's?" he asked.

"How could I miss it? It was the biggest and choicest. I didn't realize you'd be here," I said.

"Every year, twice a year, we're on display. After all, I oversee the finished product. Say, Resa, do you have some time? Maybe we could talk a few minutes?"

I really didn't think I could stop and talk with my mind on the last of rush hour congestion and a hundred mile hike back up the ascending mountains. The lights in the big hall were starting to blink off and the crowd had thinned considerably. Couples and singles were striding out the double doors as the security guards bid the convention goers a "good evening."

"Have you had dinner, Resa?" he asked

"No, just a taste of some of the samples here," I said.

"There's somewhere extraordinary I'd like you to try. Could you take a few minutes? It's not far. We could talk and catch up on the way."

The conflict was momentary and justified in my mind. Accepting a dinner date with Roland would trump the slow crawl through bumper to bumper traffic that would not thin until many miles far north of the city. So I said, "Yes."

✦✦✦✦✦✦✦✦✦✦

We strolled around the fountain adorned with the horse sculptures galloping from the foam in Old Scottsdale towards Stetson Drive and past Cowboy Ciao. Roland still hadn't revealed just where we were going but left the description of "unprecedented" to my imagination. I was keen to try a place unknown to me and given such an endorsement by a fellow food lover. I fancied myself as being "in the know" here in Scottsdale.

As we stepped into SeeSaw, I recognized the chef, Nobu, from his other restaurant a few miles north at Hapa's, where I had enjoyed the chef's individual style.

"Have you ever been here, Resa?" Roland asked, as we sat at the tiny open sushi bar.

"No, but I've heard reviews that it is good," I said.

"Good is an understatement," Roland chuckled. "More like supreme genius, inexpressible flavors and combinations: consummate madness and skill! I think you'll be pleased," he said.

What was pleasing was the fact we had the opportunity to share some time and get to know one another outside of the eyes and ears of the coffee shop.

Nobu personally greeted us and he acknowledged our familiar faces. Now that he was fully in charge of his own establishment, he could give free rein to his style and art.

As Roland explained, "Nobu is also highly regarded for his sensitivity in pairing specific wines to his creations. Let's try the *Omakase*, the tasting menu. *Omakase* means trust."

"And who should be trusted, you or Nobu?" I flirted. Roland just answered with a smile. The service was individual, personal, and whimsically attended to by Nobu himself. He took great pains in preparing each luscious morsel.

The cold edaname soup was graced with a ginger flavored crème fraiche and was savored while I heard of Roland's career struggles and successes. The hamachi was a shock of pure pleasure when combined with a grapefruit segment and an avocado slice. And the *Foss Marai Prosecco* added a citrus note needed to make the texture and flavors on my tongue unforgettable. As the small, gastronomic miracles arrived one after another on our plates, I was unable to tell if it was the companion, the conversation or the extraordinary morsels that raised the mood. We were giggling, ooohing, aaahing, blushing, and relishing combinations I never imagined. We ended with a *foie gras* marinated in *miso*, accompanied by tiny organic vegetables and a *Royal Tokaji*. I was delirious with the exciting flavor thrills. Roland was pleased with himself and the genuine effect he had in delighting me.

After closing, we ambled the darkened streets towards Buckboard Avenue and the parked cars. We were exhilarated on the experience we had shared. As we turned the corner and I started to hold out my hand and thank Roland for the evening and the consummate experience we had shared, with faces flushed, he drew me towards him and shared a warm, moist kiss of dessert. It was only natural that my arms embraced him and I was lost in kissing him back. As I felt his hot cheek slide against mine, he kissed the very dangerous side of my neck. His neroli blossom cologne drove me insane while thoughts of chocolate flooded my brain.

♦♦♦♦♦♦♦♦♦♦

I crossed paths with Barry on the highway the next morning on my way to clock in for the early shift at the clinic. Barry was entering the parking lot of the coffee shop and I knew he spotted "Work Horse" heading north to the clinic instead of south from my home. I pulled into the Medical Clinic's parking lot and grabbed a clean shirt from the back seat. I attempted a quick change since no one was in sight. Just as I pulled off yesterday's shirt, I heard the roar of a gas burner and looked up in horror to see the slow passage of a hot air balloon basket and six pairs of laughing eyes watching my disrobing. This was becoming a regular show. The tourists were skimming treetops as they floated away adding another spectacle to their Sedona vacation.

As I hastily pulled on my shirt, I decided then and there that there would be no conversation about my evening: no lies but also no cover-up. Barry was my employee and not my boyfriend, so I planned to maintain a silence about the trip and my early morning arrival.

Chapter 25

MY CELL PHONE WAS on vibration and the red light was blinking in my lab coat pocket. It was mid-morning at the Medical Clinic and I was busy. The mammography patients were scheduled every thirty minutes all day. They were lovely ladies, often asking questions about their breast health or sharing sad stories about sisters, moms, or friends. Sometimes they needed some extra understanding and time to get over the tears before we could get to the exam.

Everyone at the coffee shop had been warned never to call me when I was at the clinic, unless it was a real emergency. At lunchtime, I checked the calls left on voicemail.

"Resa, I had to close the coffee shop. Noxious fumes

made Gordon and a customer vomit and pushed us out of there. It's bad...call you later!" Click.

The coffee shop closed on a weekday? I felt an ominous rush of fear hearing about the new disaster.

Even with fans blowing non-stop, the coffee shop stayed closed for two days. Barry snooped around and found out the Institute for the Indigene was responsible. We couldn't figure out what the" I.I." was going to be and other than a work crew and one supervisor there was no one on the premises. The construction boss just followed his orders building out the space with his blueprints in hand.

When I arrived at the coffee shop, Ned had my favorite drink ready with an image of a cactus floating in the *crema*. He practiced with pictures such as the skyline of Sedona, a roadrunner, or my name spelled out in the foam.

"Oh, no. Today I'd like a hot honey Kona latte," I said.

Barry moved right in. "Not your favorite, a cold caramel macchiato?"

"No, a hot honey Kona latte," I answered.

"But you always have the cold, caramel..," he trailed off.

"A- real- hot- honey- Kona- latte," I repeated.

"Oh, I get it," Barry answered, as he nodded to Ned to change my order.

He walked away and got busy with some paperwork on the back orders. When he returned he was cool and all business.

"There's some bad news. It looks like our pal, Stein,

has sold us out. Some kind of deli is going in next door."

"Deli," I stammered, "That means sandwiches, coffee drinks, salads—it's what we do…"

"What'd you expect? He'd sell the gold outta Grandma's teeth," he retorted sarcastically.

"But, but he told us he wouldn't put competition in the building."

"He couched that remark by saying, 'But a Chinese restaurant wouldn't be direct competition,' remember… my little Matzo Ball."

"Oh, Barry, this is no time for jokes."

Breaking into a perfect Groucho Marx impersonation, an imaginary cigar wagging in his hand, Barry cracked, "Who's joking, my dear, this is a real calamity!"

◆◆◆◆◆◆◆◆◆◆

Late that evening after closing, Barry and I sat in the small back room office of the coffee shop. It was nearly 9:00 PM. We'd long ago closed for the night and completed the daily cleanup. For the last hour, we'd been slowly and cautiously going over the books. At the end of the desk, I sat separating receipts, bills, and miscellaneous expenses. Behind me, Barry added figures into a calculator while scratching notations onto a sheet of paper.

"Okay, we've got the three thousand covered for this month," said Barry. "That's the major headache. Now doctor, let's see how much it's going to take to pay off the utilities and payroll. If the patient survives, we'll go over that stack of minor expense bills you've got."

Sliding a sheet of statistics to him, I leaned back and arched my back, stretching my aching muscles. "Do companies purposely make these chairs uncomfortable?"

"Office chairs are made in factories by blue collar workers who resent the management types they're building them for. I don't know, what do you think?" Barry smiled.

"If we could just get Stein to re-negotiate the lease, it'd take a lot of pressure off," I suggested.

"He'd be glad to negotiate, as long as it resulted in higher payments. I'd sooner negotiate a soup bone from a starving pit bull," Barry replied, as he continued to work.

"He's not the most flexible person I've ever met. I'll give you that," I said.

"Not the most flexible, that's the understatement of the century. That cheapskate wouldn't throw a drowning man a life jacket unless he paid for it in advance."

"He's not that bad," I said.

"Yeah, right! I'd kick him in the heart, but I'd break my toe," he answered.

"Here, take a look at these," I said, handing him the payroll stats.

"What the heck is this from? Gordon put down eight hours of overtime last Wednesday. He didn't even work that day."

Smiling, I explained, "He told me he got a flat pulling into the parking lot. Then he had to go get the tire fixed and mounted."

"That doesn't take sixteen hours."

"Hold on, it gets better," I said. "He says he hurt his back changing the tire and had to get a massage. Then he needed to lie down to recuperate so he went to the drugstore for an over-the-counter sleeping pill."

"What does any of this have to do with all these overtime hours?" asked Barry.

"He says that because the tire went flat in our lot, we're responsible for everything that happened after that. So he wrote it up as time at work and overtime."

"So because the skin on that rubber band he calls a tire finally deflated in our lot we're responsible to take care of his bill from," Barry held up the receipt to read it closer, "From the Rub-A-Dub-Dub Massage Parlor and an x-rated video store?"

"Of course not," I laughed. "I just wanted you to see that one."

"What's next, he gets a cough and we get a bill for overtime while he goes to the Bahamas to get some sunshine to get over it?" asked Barry.

"Well, if that made the hair on your neck stand on end, this ought to make it curl up," I told him. I handed him a worn, half ripped receipt.

"This is written on a cocktail napkin," he complained.

I nodded and replied, "Keep reading."

"It's hard to read through the liquor ring," he said, squinting to read the washed out lettering. "It's for a margarita for a business necro-phili-a-tions?" he said quizzically.

"He's trying to say 'negotiations,'" I explained.

"I don't have my language dictionary, alcohol to sober version. Do you understand any of this?" he asked.

"It's a drink tab from Gerry. I want to pay it," I said.

"Of course we won't. It's ridiculous. We're not...you want to do what?" he yelped in a double take.

"I want to pay it."

"Don't let me diminish that caregiver complex of yours, but it might set a bad precedent if it gets around that the employees can go bar-hopping on the boss's dime," he warned.

"Gerry saw a whole group of folks sitting at the patio at the Town Center. They were wondering where to go to get something healthy to eat. He went in, had a drink, and brought them over here. I think we can reimburse him for a drink for that, don't you?"

"Okay, but next time have him ask the bartender for an actual receipt. This might not go over well with an I.R.S. auditor," Barry answered.

"Good."

"I'd hate to see what he'd write it on if he'd met these people at a public washroom," he said.

"How much more before we can wrap this up?" I asked.

He scribbled a few figures on his note pad. "I've still got a few figures to add in but it looks like we've driven the dreaded horde away from the palace gates for at least one more day."

I rose from my chair and said, "I'll make us each one

last coffee while you finish that."

"Oh, I work while you take a break. Is that it?"

"That's it. I'm going to take a big five minute break to make us a fancy coffee before you go home to your cozy bed and I go put in eight hours of call at the hospital."

"You're doing the night shift tonight? Why didn't you say something? I would've let you take off an hour ago," Barry exclaimed. "How in the world are you going to stay on your feet at work after the hours here? What are you going to get maybe five hours of sleep tonight? That's crazy."

"I'll be okay," I told him. "Remember, that job pays for this job. At least right now it does."

"That might be, but does it pay for your upcoming heart attack or impending stroke?" he asked.

"It's not like I wouldn't recognize the signs of anything serious. I am in the medical field, remember."

"Yeah, and so were Drs. Mengele, Kevorkian and Quakenbush. I wouldn't trust their judgment either, if I were you." He said.

"Who's Quakenbush?" I questioned.

"He's a Groucho Marx creation. No doubt before your time and not your taste in humor," he explained.

"Whatever. I've got to do it. I really don't have a choice."

Barry stood and put a hand on my shoulder. "If I could work the shift for you, I would."

"You know," I said seriously, "I believe you would."

"Yeah," he said with a theatrical drool, "Topless

women in film."

"Stop it, be respectful," I gave him a small slap for emphasis. "Tonight's shift is just covering the E.R."

He answered with a ghoulish laugh.

I turned and left without another word. As I got to my car, I let my head drop against the steering wheel. I was exhausted and now had to decide if I was being determined or just stubborn. I guess it really didn't matter because there was no turning back now. Can I hold out for two more years at this pace was the worry on my mind.

Chapter 26

S o I was torn about the fate of the coffee shop as I watched Lacey fall in love with Jim and with Sedona. She was having fun helping out at the café, but she and Jimmy were in love. They went on mountain bike rides, hikes, and threw small parties for their newly acquired friends. They were calling Sedona their own little slice of Heaven.

She brought me more news about the Business Brainstormers. One new idea was a "First-Timer Kit for Teens." It contained all the products they would need during their time transitioning from virgins to newly indoctrinated lovers. It would be marketed in a tastefully packaged, zippered pouch with a plain brown wrapper treatment. The reasoning was that girls had just barely gotten used to the menses and boys were too shy to buy their own products for sexual exploration. Suggested names were "U-Can-trol" or "Safe-Time."

Another enterprising idea was to rehabilitate the hundreds of airplanes in the old Air Force graveyard in Tucson for firefighting. The logic was: if you could get across the country in five hours or less, why not dispatch a fleet of aircraft to douse the flames while they were small.

There was talk of electric motors added to the existing gas guzzling cars, cisterns, and rain barrels to catch rainwater and much solar-panel talk. The Tin Foil Hat Lady, Eloise, sat in the last meeting with charts and graphs and scientific diagrams. She had a plan to scope all the harmful rays in a home or office and owned the gadgets to accomplish the task. The lady was a soldier with a Gauss meter and an old 1950's Civil Defense Geiger counter. She championed against the exposure of alpha, beta, gamma, and microwaves. Her plan was to track down the radon and electro-magnetic fields and make the client a blueprint of dangerous areas. Su Ling Chow, our resident Feng Shui Master, teamed up with her. They were going to offer the service to Sedona residents first. Eloise ordered her gadgets from a science catalogue and was a walking physics experiment.

Everyone was happy about the coffee shop. The Filipino boys were eating well now that I made them their own private crock-pot of pork barbeque whenever I began a posole cook-off. They loved their jobs at the coffee shop and brought their family and friends. A rag-tag poetry and musical group was meeting and performing after hours now and Barry had some fun as the Master of Ceremonies as he quipped some of his old jokes. The Intergalactic Space Travelers group faithfully met every week and talked about alien visitations. Even one of the town's councilwomen had given a gracious compliment about the "service to the City of Sedona" that the lively business had brought to the West End. As far as we were concerned, Barry and I were fully functioning and alive but exhausted robots. We were averaging a gross of ten to twelve thousand dollars a month in sales.

But my re-occurring chest pains and sleeplessness caused me to want to know that everything was all right, health wise, and that it was just stress that would pass. Every time I was asked to perform an EKG on a patient at the Medical Clinic, I tried to figure out a way to do a quick listen to my own ticker. Somehow, between being too busy and knowing it was against rules and unethical, the wish just remained unfulfilled.

"You and Zelda are gonna have to start baking," Barry made the announcement. "Miss Dipti Yogini, the Priestess of love and sugarless sweet cakes, has quit! She and Ranjit are through. They're splitting up. Oh, and by the way, Ranjit's becoming a creep; he's been hitting on the nineteen-year-old cashier at the bookstore."

"No problem, just up our orders from the Danish Pastry Company until I make other plans. I can keep plenty of cookies and brownies on the shelf," I said.

"But Barry..." I was wondering aloud, "What are all

those diabetic javalinas and coyotes going to do without their dessert behind Dipti's Delectible Bakery?"

"Reckon they'll be madder than Hell," he replied.

Chapter 27

YOU KNOW WHAT A javelina, nopalito, jalapeño burrito is, guys?" I was in a rare mood to tease and play a little with the brothers.

"No, but it sounds good, Resa," Gerry chimed in. Since his bail out, he had become a model employee. "Grateful" was the word.

"Okay, guys, this crock pot is just for you. I was just kidding about the javelina."

"Bet somebody's eaten them sometime," piped in Gordon, always the practical older brother.

"No doubt someone has tried the delicacies of the Musk Hog," I replied. "But they smell so bad and I bet that being a peccary, not a real pig, that they don't taste good. Like goat."

"Hey, goat is good. You should try some," interjected Gerry.

Flint Painted Horse came over and added to the conversation. "The hog is good eating if you skin him in the field the right way."

"What's that, Flint?" the boys chorused in unison. I could tell the brothers were intrigued.

The right way is to pull the skin over the hoof. Don't go near the scent gland. Never cut into it, spoils the meat," he said. The guys were all ears.

Grant walked out with Flint, following him to get more knowledge about this little known Arizona sport. He returned, planning to make a carne quesada or maybe a javelina chorizo per Flint's instructions.

Chapter 28

LUCKILY, MY FRIDAY AFTERNOON, the day of Queenie's dinner party, was free from the medical clinic. After her last planning visit, I learned that this was a rehearsal dinner prior to her early Saturday morning wedding ceremony held at the Spanish Chapel at Tlaquepaque.

Barry had finally given me a few more details as I had never met the woman. Thanks to Barry's casual note taking, I learned that her real name was Regina, not Queenie, and her final head count was still at thirty-five. The groom was a real Brit and would be in charge of hosting their private wine bar if we set up a table and wine glasses. The husband-to-be was flying his elderly parents in from London. I started thinking tea, really good, strong

English tea.

By my calculations, the visiting parents would be dining in the wee hours of the morning if they traveled straight across. What they would need would be an authentic black tea with dinner. There was only one choice, P.G.Tips, double strength.

For this event, I needed to supervise a little so I donned suitable attire and asked Barry to be the voice to make the welcome and any announcements or cues to begin the buffet line as necessary. Zelda would finish all of my preparations, girl power at the oven. The chicken breasts smelled heavenly. The skin was golden brown and crisping nicely as they baked. Zelda had already found my drum of parsnip and carrots; they had been simmered into a tender doneness and were cool enough to prepare the *sucre carrotte puree*, a wonderful adult baby food.

Peeping out of Zelda's deep apron pocket was a bottle of Don Julio Tequila, the best of the aged varieties, so smooth no mixer was necessary. She whispered to me in a conspiratorial way that while the guests were eating, that long, dead period of time when our work was done and before clean-up, we deserved a nip. It was a Friday night and I for one would not refute her offer.

The doors were locked at 6:00 PM. A few wanna-be customers knocked, and then discouraged by the private party sign, slinked away. The white x-ray cardboards had come in handy again.

The buffet table, set up in a corner, was beautifully arranged. I had small, folded stand-up cards with the names, in calligraphy, of each dish fronting the large serving platters. The evening would end at the barista station with a dapper Barry dispensing after-dinner coffees.

The British in-laws were every bit as jet-lagged as I had imagined. They registered true shock that a decent pot of true English tea accompanied their place setting. It revived them enough to voice a round of toasts and much good cheer.

This was going so well that during the lull, the cooks took a few nips off Zelda's bottle. As we hid in the back of the sink room steeling ourselves for the clean-up ahead, Zelda remarked, "I didn't know you knew Regina Haverford."

"Oh, I don't know her. I just met her tonight," I explained. Barry made all the arrangements. He kept calling her, Queenie. Pass me that Don Julio again, please."

"Don't you know who she is?" Zelda asked knowingly.

"She's the bride getting married tomorrow."

"Yeah, but she broadcasts an all-vegan, how-to cooking TV show from her kitchen right here in Sedona," Zelda informed me; she was in the know.

Choking, I gave Zelda back her bottle with a big, dumbfounded look on my face.

"You mean we're cooking for a T.V. chef's rehearsal dinner?"

"Yeah. Oh, and by the way, I heard that Roland's been married," she said.

As I passed the bottle back to Zenda, I remarked in a

tiny voice, "It was just a kiss."

Chapter 29

A HIKE INTO THE West Fork of the Oak Creek Canyon is stepping into a fairytale designed by Mother Nature. Morgan, the self-appointed cheesecake guru, my friend of twenty years, was a hiker and wouldn't take 'no' for an answer. I found my old Patagonia boots in the back of the closet and agreed to go. After all, I hadn't been outside much since I was always running from the coffee shop to the clinic to home and back again.

As we strode toward the creek, we passed hundred-year-old apple trees. They were the original plantings of the first settlers in Sedona. The gnarled ancients bore little fruit and emanated a powerful energy that made me feel like I was passing pillars in a temple.

"So how's it really going?" Morgan asked, striding

along.

I was huffing and puffing, hardly able to talk and hike. Maybe it took the great outdoors and a close girlfriend to come clean. The gurgling creek water was a confessional font.

"I just don't know what I got myself into, Morgan, at my age."

"You mean our age," she retorted.

"Yeah," I chuckled, "The late fifties don't feel like the new thirties with two jobs."

"Can't you quit the clinic yet?"

I had to push to just struggle behind her. "Don't dare," I gasped. "I keep putting cash into the business each month. I'm in a trap." She already knew from past girl talk about the personal guarantee, the lease, and my contract with Barry.

"What about the curse?" Morgan asked, over her shoulder. She revealed a bit of voodoo, a Sedona secret. "Didn't anyone ever tell you?"

It took me ten quick strides to get back into earshot. "Yeah, I've heard a couple of versions."

"There's a curse on the building. A lot of people know about it. Isn't Barry helping enough?" she asked.

"No matter what I say, he balks at my expansion ideas," I replied. "The coffee shop needs longer hours, dinners on weekends, and liquor." The sun was beginning to set and the shadows from the wind-swept trees were dancing on the floor of the trail. "Can't we stop and look at all this gorgeous scenery for a minute, Morgan?" I needed to catch my breath.

She answered, "Sure," but I knew she wanted to hike and not amble.

"I almost got into trouble at the clinic the other day," I said as I started into my story.

"What happened?" Morgan asked, choosing a perfectly comfortable rock to sit down.

"Well, I've been having some funny, tingly feeling pains right here." I had my right hand planted over my heart. "So the other day I decided to try an EKG on myself you know, in between patients."

"Get out! Shut up!" she replied.

"Yeah, I hiked up my scrub shirt and got all the stickers on in all the right places. I was standing up next to the machine in the back room. It only takes ten seconds to read. Getting it rigged up takes the longest."

"No kidding?" now Morgan was interested. "So what happened?"

By now I was breathing normally again, having found my own hard rock throne. "Just as I was hooking up the leads, Lisa, the lead tech, opened the door and yelled 'Resa, stat case in the ER!'"

"Then what?" Morgan was grinning from ear to ear, loyal enough to not lecture me on what an idiot I was.

"I jumped a foot high. Luckily, my back was turned to her and the door—never did get to run the strip."

"You're nuts!"

"Anyway, Morgan, I'm starting to think I should add more hours. Barry's against it. Any thoughts?"

"I hate to break the news, darling, but your G.M., Mr. General Manager, Barry, likes to have a little smokey-tokey, a left handed cigarette, some wacky-tobaccy! Get it? That could be one of your big problems."

"What can I say to him about what he does in his off-hours? He works sun-up to sun-down," I said.

The air was still. The birds were chirping an early good night to one another. "Oh, while we're on the subject of problems, Morgan, I have to talk to you about the cat hair in the cheesecakes."

"Let's talk as we're heading back. It's getting dark," she suggested.

♦♦♦♦♦♦♦♦♦♦

After the hike into West Fork, Morgan and I stopped at the Oak Creek Brewery for a fresh cold draught. The new batch of amber ale was ready to pull. Dakota and Sissy would meet us there. Dakota attracted attention everywhere she went with her spectacular beauty. Her unique style of wardrobe was a combination of Native American and 1890's cowgirl. It came across as both sexy and tribal.

Sissy was involved in a hopeful new romance that centered on singing the standards under the spotlight at the karaoke bar.

"Just a short one, Morgan," I said. "I'm heading in for some shut-eye."

The band she wanted to hear, the Daddy Up's, would be

on stage as soon as the weekly drumming session was over. The level of sound was at the upper reaches of decibels just before pain and hearing damage. The thumping vibrated into my chest as we walked into the joint.

The menagerie assembled in the cramped space was garbed in styles of every different nation, mind set, and occupation. A four and a half-foot tall, little person from Zimbabwe wore red suede boots, short pants of bright yellow, and a knitted cap adorned with threaded tassels ending in bells that chimed and flew in every direction with his ecstatic head movements.

The drummers, at least a dozen in number, maintained a steady non-stop beat on a range of skins from Congo, snare, floor toms, bongos, a bass drum, Indian tom-toms and handmade versions. The bombilations were rocking the brewery as the crowd jumped into a frenzy of deafening, thumping pulsation. There was no stopping. It was an endless flow of beats, jumps, leaps, bodies rocking, moving in cadence while the walls and the fourteen-foot high beer vats vibrated with the pounding. I wondered if the beer became vibrationally infused from the music and the drumming sessions.

The Oak Creek Amber Ale was smooth and sweet and I licked my foam mustache with relish. The drumming was deafening and after a long twenty-minute stretch, I excused myself and went back to my bungalow for rest and renewal. Sissy and Morgan, my overnight houseguests, would find their way in later in the wee hours.

As I drove home from the brewery, I realized that I

was just "no fun" and had lost the ability to endure the spectacle of the native drumming and the dancing with utter abandon that I had witnessed. I was longing for my pillow and just some peace and quiet. All I wanted to hear was the wildlife sounds. The never-ending Sedona wind whispering through pine needles was the soothing music I wanted to lull me to sleep.

Hours later, I was pulled from the clutches of a dark noisy nightmare by Sissy. She was on her knees beside me on my bed, shaking me from a sweat-drenched screeching place in my subconscious.

"Honey, you were having a bad dream. You were yelling," she said.

I started coming back from the frightening scene. As Sissy climbed in under the comforter, she started on her sermon of care and concern.

"What was going on with you? What's the matter? There's something seriously wrong, Resa."

As I rose out of the vapor shroud, the memory of my caterwaul and the scenes came back to me. After a long drink of water, I related the infernal scene I had just experienced in a world of heights, cliffs, and terror.

"The train was coming. I was tied to the tracks like in the old time movies. I got loose. Stein was chasing me." Just like an older sister, she listened. "Everyone was behind him…"

"Who?"

"My kids, my friends, you, the coffee shop crew, some customers, Barry…He had me running over rocks, near the cliffs…"

"Who?"

"Stein! Everyone was at the canyon, not Oak Creek, the Grand Canyon. I was running for miles and miles."

"Yeah."

"He was waving the lease in his hand and I was scared, really, really scared."

"Then what?"

"I tried to get away. The Sky Bridge was the only way. I ran to the far edge and he had me backed to the wall."

"The glass bridge?"

"Yeah, the glass bridge."

"They were all after me… in the dream…"

"You mean nightmare!" she corrected.

"I looked down; it was awful. I was going to jump to get away from Stein. Then you woke me up."

Sissy was quiet for a few minutes before she started. I could hear her deep intakes and quick exhales of breath, which warned me she was forming her lecture.

"That's it, that's enough of all this madness. It has to stop! Tomorrow you're going to go talk to Jack; he'll know what to do. You can't go on like this. It just isn't correct!"

Sissy stayed there a while longer speaking softly in her musical voice about the rights and wrongs in women's lives and then effortlessly slid into a blow-by-blow account of several recent dates. They were air castles of future romance filled with rainbows and poetry. I was able to slide back into sleep at the sound of her sweet murmurings.

Chapter 30

THERE ARE BLOODY FEW men in the world to trust, but a woman needs at least one.

One she respects and can believe when the time calls for an expert male opinion. In my case it is my taxman, Captain Jack McDaniels.

He was found puttering around Canyon Lake in the Solar Star 21, his latest acquisition. "Come aboard, little lady," he welcomed. I climbed onto the rocking boat leaving care behind.

"Just sold several of these in Dubai. Take a tour. They are green, green, green, and going wherever there's sun and water traffic," he explained.

Jack had had a long career in finance and saving floundering businesses. He came in and turned things around. Each time we met, I heard yet another chapter of his life, from a U.S. Air Force test pilot, to a C.F.O., to now head of a solar boat company. Even though he admitted to being in his mid-seventies, he had the looks and vitality of a fifty- year-old full of sap.

A feeling of relaxation took over after we traversed the lake and I began to pose the question of 'what should I do?' by giving Jack the long litany of coffee shop problems: slow sales, high overhead, rising coffee bean prices, new neighbors and their construction disturbances, personal health issues, a running comedy show from the general manager and now the crew—who once loved and respected me—now quaked and feared my arrival. I even complained over my split fingertips, which were sealed with a liquid bandage solution and taped tightly. They felt like a hundred deep paper cuts. I left out the news that my hand surgeon wanted to schedule a procedure that took weeks to heal.

"Jack, the crew tries to avoid me. They used to love me. I swear I never anticipated that would happen."

He just chuckled as he anchored the boat in the middle of the lake. We bobbed like apples at a Halloween Party. There was something soothing about the motion of the boat in the hot Arizona sun and the stupendous scenery viewed from the surface of the water.

"Look at it this way," he said. "You have over a year behind you, and you have a little jewel of a business."

"Humm, it's my baby," I said. "You could look at it like that."

"The numbers are good. You started with an established small business you acquired for $15K. You put another $40K of your own money into it and so far in the first year you've generated $120K against your overhead. Some people are just great at starting businesses and then putting them up for sale. No crime in that. Look at what you've got."

"Yeah, I built my own prison and the inmates hate me."

"As a model, your café could be a good example at a business course," he said.

"Maybe a good example to start a business when you're young and focused on only one job," I mused.

The boat trip to the middle of the lake made me relax for the first time in months. I had gotten away from all the worries for a while as Captain Jack put everything into his own brand of perspective.

I didn't go right back to the coffee shop after our meeting. I needed some time to sort out all that Captain Jack had said and to think about everything I had created in the last eighteen months. It had been a big project. What I needed now was some alone time; I needed a blast of Vortex energy.

One of the quickest and easiest spots to get a fix of power and strength was atop the winding hill above the city. There was one rock up there I had in mind. It was my plan to sit a spell and consult with all the earthly vibrations I could absorb. The view was magnificent, evoking a natural altered state of consciousness as the Wind shuffled against my skin. I sat on that rock a long, long time. It was situated out of sight of the throng of tourists who stood at the apex, snapping innumerable photos. It took me a few minutes to walk back up the crest and as I turned back one more time to look over this glorious undulating carved-out valley of monoliths and wonder, I made up my mind what I would do.

Chapter 31

I T WAS POLICE OFFICERS Sanders and Taylor who
partnered on the night shift in sleepy Sedona that
answered the call. They expected one of the usual
alerts for the resort town: a non-guest sleeping in his vehicle
outside one of the major resorts, a weekend warrior hiker
stuck on a ledge, an out-of-town speeder, an intoxicated
Harley bike rider weaving westward on Highway 89A, or
any one of the standard weekend calls.

The radio cracked a little, "Sanders, could you and
Taylor get over to Shelby Road right away?" Dispatcher
Collins asked.

They sat up straight in the cruiser trying to get some
blood flowing. Taylor couldn't decide whether to use the
lights and the siren. They were parked near Thunder

Mountain by the library since it was always quiet over there. Both men blinked a couple of times trying to get the order they heard sorted out. Shelby Road was all residences, consisting of a few home businesses, hardly a place for an incident. They were rare in Sedona with all the peace, love, and pot smoke.

Dispatcher Collins transferred the order clearly. "Check out a reported wildlife disturbance over there. Might need to call the Fish and Game boys. Get back to me." With lights on and no siren, the cruiser pulled out onto Dry Creek Road.

Sanders and Taylor let the cruiser crawl down Shelby like a purring mountain lion on the prowl. The windows were open to let in the warm, dry, night air and they both caught the unmistakable scent of javelina at the same time.

Checking the house numbers against Collins' air-waved address, Sanders pulled alongside the curb and killed the motor. He grabbed a flip baton and an eighteen-inch flashlight. Taylor did the same as they exited the vehicle. He left his cruiser door ajar.

"Wish I hadn't just polished these boots," Taylor lamented. "Just hate their darn scat," he talked into thin air. Sanders agreed but didn't bother to comment. He was concentrating on the rat-tat-tat, shuffling, and huffing noises he was picking up. He turned his right ear towards the fence and analyzed the sounds: a bump, then silence, now scratching, a clicking of cloven hooves, a brief greedy quibble followed by a gruff snarl. He eyeballed Taylor to head the other way to encircle the property and get a gander at the long backyard slope running into a dense arroyo of creosote, juniper, and sage. The beams of lights from their torches caught movements in the desert bushes as bristled rumps and curly tails disappeared into the shadows. There was no mistaking the odoriferous, musky stench that reeked and screamingly announced a calling card entitled "javalina herd in residence."

Sanders headed to the front door and rang the bell. Lights came on in rooms. A slight woman wearing a loud flower print housedress to her ankles, answered.

She gasped immediately, "I'm so glad you're here!"

She hunched her shoulders and looked toward the back of the house. "They're out there; they won't leave. I'm scared to death." Her voice rose to a squeal. "You can't believe what they're doing." Dipti Yogini, a.k.a. Betty Mayer, was clinging onto the screen door and cowering at the same time.

"Now, Ma'am, the javelina can't hurt you. Nuisance is all. They'll be gone in a few minutes. We'll take a look out back if that's okay with you."

Dipti was distressed. "Make them go away; you don't understand. They're trying to GET IN!"

Sanders and Taylor had heard and seen a lot of things in their respective careers, but in Sedona, the pigs preferred the great outdoors and belonged far from town in the backcountry. The officers exchanged a knowing look that said Betty, a.k.a. Dipti, must have been sampling a little too much of the smoky *shesh*a pipe or too many nips of the juice of the agave. Sanders used his educated nose for a whiff of a Saturday night tipple but only detected the aromatic wafts of baked goods, household cleaning products, and an earlier dinner of pot roast. A flood of cold, air-conditioned air floated out the door.

"Is anyone else home, Ma'am?" Now it was Taylor's chance to get involved.

"No," Dipti admitted tearfully. "I'm alone."

"Can you call anyone to come over?" he asked gently.

"Maybe," she sniffled.

"We'll check out back, Ma'am. I'll let you know what we find." Before he could turn and leave, Dipti added, "They're looking in the window, in the back room by my bakery…" She sounded like a loon.

Creeping back to the fence, both officers felt no fear. Desert pigs rarely come near homes since they prefer to roam and exist on a diet of roughage, cactus pads, and the sour autumn fruit of the napalitos. Javelinas don't venture too close, not unless someone feeds them. As they crept behind the added-on room that housed the bakery, they saw a sight they would never forget.

"Gosh darn," rasped Sanders under his breath.

Taylor croaked a "What in all blue blazes?"

In a cooperative effort, three javelinas were stacked, windowsill high, one atop another, in a balancing act rivaling a Ringling Brothers circus display. The top dog in this charade sat on his buddies' shoulders and used his front paw to scratch repeatedly at the bakery window.

The lights from the cop's torches startled the trio: the

three little piggies. As the beams flooded a casting search down the slope, a sea of shining eyeballs looked back with hungry, angry looks.

"Whee, by golly," said Taylor, "Did you ever see so many hogs in one place?" The acrobatic trio had now jumped down with embarrassment and jogged off to rejoin their herd, their tails and scent sending a snobbish retreat.

Sanders surveyed the melee with his flashlight. Amongst the crowd, he spotted a half dozen coyotes, big and well fed instead of the wily, slinky, skinny variety. These were as sleek as German shepherd show dogs.

"Curious as all get out, Taylor," he remarked. "Coyotes never run with hogs!"

As the beams from the police flashlights revealed the displaced herd, they spooked. Frightened, angry, frustrated, and hungry for their missing treats, they ran to the far right of the sloping yard, heading north through a break in the hedgerow and unfortunately directly towards the center of town.

Both officers juked towards the stream of wildlife now heading for the front of Shelby Road and out of Dipti's back yard. They could not move fast enough or wall off the galloping line of pigs that leapt over the trampled fence. They were now set free.

The main police station on Sundowner Avenue was besieged with telephone calls by midnight. Complaints came in from the front desk at the Rouge Resort. There was a sighting from a merchant in Uptown. A couple of scared

French speaking tourists spotted the herd and snapped a photo. An angry *maitre' de* at the fancy Italian restaurant on Gunslinger Street shooed the pesky hogs away from his parking lot. There were countless calls from the ordinary citizens. Now there was a report from the security guard at the Hilton. There was a javelina in the hot tub. Collins was hearing insane reports of romping, snuffling musk hogs and noisy coyotes. A dog had been accosted sexually. Garbage cans were overturned. Someone was calling in on a cell-phone; it seems an army of wildlife was galloping down Highway 89A. Some had clotheslines dragging and bits of underwear trailing behind.

As Sanders and Taylor heard the radio in the cruiser squawk them to attention they backed off a few feet and decided to call for backup.

"Get Bobby Begay and Flint Painted Horse on this, too." Sanders yelled into his cell-phone. "We're gonna need help."

As they exited Dipti's backyard, the officers saw a couple of pigs lounging in the prowler.

Chapter 32

MILES FROM SEDONA UNDER the light of a glorious full moon, Bobby Begay and Flint Painted Horse were squatting close to their campfire. The firelight was reflected in the big, kind eyes of their mounts tethered nearby. Flint had some upscale gear close at hand: his Coleman lantern, a cast iron skillet, a campfire coffeepot, two cups, and a half-pound of green coffee beans.

The fire had burned for several hours and died down to a bed of red-hot coals perfect for roasting the beans that would have the faint smoky taste the old-time pioneers called, cowboy coffee. Grunting a little from his squat, Flint settled into a small camp chair and shook the cast iron skillet. He carefully watched the beans roast. As he hummed a rhythmic Native American chant he was intently listening for the first crack.

In Navaho, Bobby asked his friend, "Doesn't it just make you madder than all get-out that they call what our people taught them, cowboy coffee?"

Shaking the pan to make the roast even, Flint replied also in tongue, "Heck no, I'm used to all their thievery. I know that we taught them how to roast the bean."

"It's good to do the old ways," Bobby said, waiting patiently with the antique grinder at the ready.

Flint was involved with the ritual. "I treat every single coffee as its own entity."

Out of respect, Bobby nodded agreement and let Flint go on. They were enjoying the smells of the coffee bean's progress to roasted perfection in the chill of the night air.

"There is an inner essence from the Earth, a natural spirit, in each bean," Flint whispered. The sound of the shaking beans made a whispery music in the night air.

Bobby wanted to help the ceremony along, so he rattled the rain stick for emphasis.

Flint continued, "This is an exercise in getting closer to the Fire Dance which is released at the second crack."

Bobby interjected approval with guttural sounds of, "Uggg," as he roasted a couple of plump marshmallows over the campfire. As Bobby blew out the flames on his burning dessert and handed a hot one over to Flint, a cell phone rang. Bobby grunted a greeting and listened as the fire sputtered. Flint was busy grinding the fragrant hot beans, ready to add to the boiling water when Bobby related the message, now back to English.

"Taylor just called and needs help rounding up about thirty head of javelina and coyotes before they hit Uptown," Bobby said, still holding the cell phone to his ear.

"What are they doing over there?" asked Flint. "They belong behind the ridge past Cathedral Rock," he continued, mostly to himself. He was performing coffee alchemy with the precision of a chemist.

"Yeah," Bobby spoke into the cell phone. "We'll help; we're on our way."

"Not before we have our coffee, my friend. It's an estate grown Brazilian, a fine Arabica bean from the Marquesde Paiva," Flint remarked, handing Bobby a cup.

◆◆◆◆◆◆◆◆◆◆

Back on Shelby Road, Sanders and Taylor were helpless to do more than track the wildly running pig herd. What had started out to be another sleepy shift was now a tension-filled chase after sugar-crazed hogs galloping amok where they didn't belong.

Miles from town Bobby Begay and Flint Painted Horse loaded up all their gear in their saddlebags.

"Think you got enough ammo, Bobby?" asked Flint.

Bobby showed him a gigantic bag of marshmallows and smiled, "No problem." He had his plastic gun loaded. As they mounted up and rode over the ridge and back toward the lights of town, they just couldn't help but wheel the horses and let out a couple of war whoops.

Chapter 33

Ɪɴ ᴛʜᴇ ᴍᴏʀɴɪɴɢ ᴛʜᴇ winds scuttled up and clanged the brass Arcosanti bells to annoyance level. I had to find a ladder to bring the noisy bells inside. For weeks, the never resting winds blew in from the northwest until nerves were on edge. A layer of pork scented fog hung over the valley. A wisp of smoke was inching straight up from Songbird Trailer Court also known as Little Mexico.

As I arrived at the coffee shop, a tall thirty-something man was leaving. He had that familiar, 'but I just can't place him' face. A toothpick was at the corner of his mouth, barely hanging on to the lower lip. The pretty blonde at his side fairly skipped along. As they passed, they were smiling and making whispered plans. Lovers,

I thought. On second thought, was that one of the young chefs featured on the *Food Channel?*

Bobby and Flint were already sitting at their corner table chowing down on the breakfast burritos.

"Kinda early for you two, isn't it?" I asked.

"Been up all night."

"Can I get you a coffee," I asked.

"Got some right here," Flint replied, tapping the shiny thermos beside his arm.

"Oh, I get it…B.Y.O.B.

"Ever have cowboy coffee? Flint asked. You don't know what you're missing."

Bobby added with a sly grin, "It's Navaho style."

"I'll pass but I am curious," I said. Bobby just winked.

The Business Brainstormers filed in for another meeting at the coffee shop for Phillip's special presentation. All of them were now wearing shiny tin-foil hats. I caught bits and pieces of Phillip's project. By now, the Brainstormers were a source of stimulation and their ideas were good fodder for some contemplation.

"My presentation today, ladies and gentlemen, is one for obliterating world hunger," he began. There were murmurs of approval all around.

"Simply, the Third World Nations are starved for amino acids and proteins to produce healthy brain tissue for the new generations. As some of you already know from my last lecture, there are fifty-some species of hare in the world. Some farm rabbits weigh out to twenty pounds or more. The rabbit is one animal that can gain weight ounce for ounce depending on what it's fed. Phillip's voice carried well in the vaulted space.   He summed it up: rabbits raised on offshore, floating rafts, fed with seaweed and grain. He proposed a chain of burger joints to feed the hungry with his Bunny Burgers. Consider the spin-off products, the marketing...fur coats, a secondary crop of trout and oysters, raised under the rafts.

The weather looked promising if the mist burned off. The air smelled like good old North Carolina barbeque. Now I spotted a second trail of smoke crawling skyward. Somewhere in town someone was roasting flesh with a porky aroma.

As I started my shift, my assistant manager, Ned, reminded me that my accountant, Mr. Sterling, had confirmed by phone that he expected me at 10:00AM for our appointed meeting. The purpose was a review of the first year's financials: a compendium of the coffee shop's performance. This was a meeting I both welcomed and dreaded. Ned comforted me with another of his barista extravaganzas; my name was floating atop the crème of a special brew he made me. It was served in one of the pint-sized mugs that dished up the soups and stews. The Weathervane logo was imprinted on the face of the soup mug. Small foamy hearts and tiny flower shapes framed my name. Ned had learned to kiss ass in the military.

I was grateful Gordon had agreed to this one Saturday morning shift. He squeezed in as many shifts around his tattoo appointments as he could, spreading his art and sustaining his income. His offer of a free tat for me hung in the air like a gift of herpes, once contracted, never leaving.

The skin artist—a map of ink—sauntered up as I began another batch of Italian wedding soup.

"Resa, those last customers were strange," he stated.

"Strange in what way, Gordon?" I was interested and starved for news.

"Well, it's still early, not lunch time yet."

"Ah, huh," I agreed, checking the time.

"They didn't order breakfast, went straight for lunch," he said.

"A lot of people on vacation are here from the East Coast, Gordon. It's the time difference of three hours. Even the internationals are all in a zone, time wise…" I explained.

"No, you don't get it," he interjected. "They ordered one of everything on the menu and kept saying they wanted the cactus and the prickly pear dishes. They'd take a bite or two and go on to the next dish. I did my best," he motioned to the trail of dishes spread out over the work area. "Their bill was huge-moneous!" Spoken with a Tagalog accent. That was a funny word. For a second, I wondered how he added it to his English vocabulary.

"I gotta take a cigarette break—I'll be out back," Gordon said. It wasn't possible to argue with him when he was in this mood.

Strange was all I thought until a brilliant flash crossed my mind. I rummaged for the itemized credit card slip in the register drawer. It would contain a signature; there had been a vaguely familiar face. The scrawl on the slip was an illegible flourish. But that familiar face continued to haunt me.

Before leaving for the appointment with the accountant, I pushed the step ladder up close to reach a high shelf above the sink to bring down some unused dishes since I wanted to get them ready for the expanded hours. As I shakily picked up a heavy stack of china, a flood of old dishwater and the bodies of drowned cockroaches mixed into a fermented, soupy slurry poured down onto my head.

♦♦♦♦♦♦♦♦♦♦

Millennium Financial was a two-person operation: Steven and Peggy Sterling, husband and wife, happily married. My appointment was promptly at ten in the morning. My private reserve of Dominican Republic coffee beans provided a freshly brewed cup for each of us. I couldn't help but notice the smoky aroma of manzanita wood wafting in the air. Something in the air smelled delicious just like barbequed spare ribs. I was born with a nose for scent and an oral curiosity, alas, no head for numbers.

The Millennium Financial Service was chosen to supplement Barry's meticulous recordkeeping. I made it quite clear there would be no under-the-table transactions or double set of cooked books. So far, the only cooking was done on the griddle. Coffee in hand, I settled into the small waiting room as Peggy announced my arrival.

After a quick hello, Steve got right to it, handing me his synopsis.

"Not bad for the first year, Ms. Milan, but don't quit your day job, at least not yet," he stated.

"Can't even think about that," I replied, looking and listening as intently as possible hoping to glint a secret to success from my bean counter.

"The biggest problem here is the rent," Steve was pointing to a fat column of numbers. "Way too high." He was shaking his head and tut, tut, tutting.

"Rent should only be five to eight percent of budget, not eighteen to twenty percent." It was late in the game for that instruction. I pursed my lips and listened.

"Right here, food costs are in line, aha, good," he nodded. At least something was right.

"Can you cut staff at all?" he asked.

"We operate with a skeleton crew. Get them off the clock as soon as possible. They're all part-timers."

"How long will the G.M. continue on this low salary?" he asked.

"We have a separate agreement. Barry will get partial ownership after each consecutive year and a share of profits," I answered.

"Will he assume a similar share of the liabilities?" Steve asked.

"I'll check the contract on that."

"Could you renegotiate the amount of rent with the landlord, now that the building's filling up? I'd get him to come down on these CAM's or cancel them all together since the other tenants are paying that, too. That would help a little," he advised.

The CAM's, Common Area Maintenance fees, had been on the shoulders of the coffee shop for a year now. With the addition of the new neighbors, Stein actually raised the CAM's.

"Why not divide them evenly with the new Latvian Deli, the Institute and the other new upstairs neighbors?" He looked at me over his glasses.

"I'll give that a try," I said

"Next, you've got to raise your prices twelve to fifteen percent across the board. No bones about it," he stated.

I sunk down in my chair an inch and groaned. To raise prices now on my loyal customers, the locals, would be embarrassing.

"So what are your plans to justify the rent? When are you going to evening hours?"

"As soon as possible. I'm working on that and some other expanded services such as..." I reeled off the things I'd been arguing with Barry about. The only way to get around this was to meet it head on and go through it. As my Grandpa had always said, "*Start out like you can keep up!*"

"Does everything look in order, I mean, the monthly reports you get from the coffee shop?" I asked.

"Clean as a whistle," he announced. "It's neither good nor bad," he mused. "You're just not making money. You're just breaking even on the day-to-day operations. You'll need to pay the G.M. a real salary and pay yourself.

Don't want the IRS taking a second look."

"Yeah, I'd love to get paid some day."

"A business like this is really hard the first few years," he countered. "At least you have one thing, a lot of losses for your tax return this year."

Chapter 34

THAT EVENING I SHARED a home-cooked meal with Jimmy and Lacey. We sat at my heavy wooden, oak table which easily seated eight. It was also a great space for cards, gambling, and board games. We were feeling like family and since I'd known Jimmy during his teenage years, it was seeing his metamorphosis into an accomplished young man that was intriguing. Now he was calling all the shots in his life and very possibly becoming a couple with Lacey.

During dessert, while we forked mounds of Aunt Virginia's moist cinnamon- scented apple cake into our mouths, the conversation turned to the café: the good, the bad, and the ugly. I started to break the news about what the accountant had reported to me. For the first time, I communicated my concerns and the weight of all I had pulled down upon my own head. I even mentioned the "Curse" though I wasn't a superstitious person. The last fact was that the green coffee bean prices had risen again and the costs were being passed directly down. The bean prices were up to $6.28 a pound.

Lacey literally jumped out of her chair. "I know what we need, Mom," she voiced her authority, "a blessing of the business. You never got one when you moved in."

"What's all that about?" I asked. My thoughts spun back to when I was a little girl. The priest would come to our aunt's house to bless it, throwing holy water all around from the gold shaker he carried. And then on Holy Saturday, women would take their baskets of paska, kielbasa, cooked eggs, and Ukrainian nut rolls to the church to be blessed before the Easter Sunday morning breakfast.

"When I was still in New York, I called you and told you to do it, a blessing," she reminded me. "You never did…"

"No, but at this point, I'm willing to try anything."

As Barry let himself in the back door to join the discussion and have a slice of cake, an aroma of Eau de Hemp trailed in after him. I made a mental note to have a private conversation with him afterward.

"Don't worry, Mom, I'll take care of all the arrangements. You don't have to do a thing," Lacey offered. "No, we'll invite the new neighbors and make it a little party!" She was already planning.

"What's this all about?" Barry asked.

"We're going to have the café blessed!" she said.

"Birkhat Ha-Gomel," announced Barry.

Chapter 35

THE DATE FOR THE *Puja* was set and handwritten invitations were passed out to the Latvian deli owners, Bookstore Pete and his wife Amy, eight of our loyal customers, Dipti and Ranjit, now back on speaking terms and, of course, the crew of loyal employees including Zelda.

The Wat Dhammaviraa Temple of Divine Being sent three nuns and one monk at sundown on the Friday of the ceremony. Two of the nuns had been customers at the café many times always choosing only the vegetarian items. Their saffron robes were in the Tibetan style and within minutes a small altar indicating their practice was set up with holy items: fruit, burning incense, water, and a bouquet of roses. The Blessed Rice had a special place centered on the altar.

Lacey had been instrumental in encouraging and organizing the ceremony and had visited the nearby Temple which also had a *stupa* on the grounds. To enhance our ceremony, which would include a parade, she had assembled a prayer bowl, a bell-shaped clapper, a gong with mallet, and packets of birdseed and rose petals. To welcome our officiants, Lacey had hung multi-colored prayer flags across the doors. The squares were in bright hues and imprinted with gold Tibetan symbols and letters. A horse decorated with plumes was stamped on each fluttery paper.

Zelda helped me set up a table for the light dinner to follow. To make the small group feel festive, the bright pink, prickly pear lemonade stood waiting in a cut glass punch bowl.

Accompanied by murmurs and scraping sounds, the chairs were arranged in a wide circle without fanfare or instruction. The guests weightlessly floated into their seats facing the altar. The nuns and the monk sitting side by side in a row were a pumpkin-colored wall of quiet energy. Voices were hushed; all eyes pulled toward the spiritual magnet that the sitting Buddhists became. We grew into a collective silence. A note card containing the chosen names and the correct pronunciation of the local Temple was handed to me. I rose to announce that we would be welcoming Sister Japti who would lead the *Puja*.

As the ceremony began, a palpable vibration emanated from the four holy disciples of Buddha. There was less air in the room and a sound of winged insects in eardrums. Japti explained the purpose of the *Puja*; we all listened with rapt attention. She spoke of emotional blockage, of a dispirited emotion, and of feelings that were too coarse. The purpose of the ceremony was to remove the disharmony that may have lodged within the space. The Buddha, we learned, welcomed prosperity and harmony for a place of commerce. These prayers would be released by the chanting of the four holy ones and by our participation.

A path of transformation would heal the space. There would be several parts to the ceremony: the Chanting, Imploring Lord Buddha, the Removing, a Silence, and a Refining of Positive Energy. Devotional moods to liberate the energy were necessary. We were all confounded but going along with it anyhow.

Then the next nun in the line-up, Sister Mona, rose and passed out a printed version of the chants we would hear. This was so we could follow along in English. No one knew what to expect and the small group of guests were as well behaved as children waiting for a sweet treat. A petition to the Buddha followed in English:

> "With fool no company keeping,
> With the wise ever consorting,
> To the worthy Homage paying,
> This is the Highest Blessing.
> Oh mani padme, Ohm."

The four voices slowly became a chorus of polyphonic

tones, melding into one sound that rose and fell and did not stop or falter for a full half-hour. At first I followed along, reading the prayers and keeping place with the liquid diggery-do voices.

Soon I was lost, completely unable to find a place in the translated words. I let go of the search to follow the prayers. I just began to listen to the fleeting oaths and sitting on that chair, began to spin into the sound.

Soon, I experienced a rise and fall and whirled into a dizzy state until I felt intoxicated. As the minutes passed, the intonation became a golden bridge of sound that transported all of us into a different drugged state. When the cadence finally stopped, many minutes later, drooping heads slowly rose back from a sleepy place of mottled consciousness.

Handfuls of the blessed rice were cast about the four corners of the room by the nun named, Sister Miranda. The monk, Brother Keinda, now gave the dazed participants instructions to travel to every part of the building, every floor, every nook and cranny, and to cast the rice, the seeds and the petals. Feelings of love must be present and words of harmony, prosperity, and hope must be spoken as we did this.

The parade began. At first we shyly followed the orange robed devotees and copied their motions. Now the guests flung the rice and commanded sweet thoughts to replace the constipation.

"Come back, harmony! Fill the space with love and welcome love. Invite prosperity. Out with evil, stagnation, the curse, obstruction, and grief. Out with loss, with death. Out with the past, with discourse, feuds, and greed."

A crack in the universe was opening and we were about to bring change. We wandered every part of the building and the grounds: every square inch. The participants were now splintering off in singles and straggling twos and threes. We crisscrossed paths and now the clouds were lifting and we were smiling and laughing. We were shouting for PROSPERITY, AGREEMENT, ORDER, UNION, LOVE, UNDERSTANDING, and HAPPINESS!

Nearly an hour later, the guests wandered back to the dining room, empty-handed, having cast the blessings into the all corners. A weight was gone. The curse was banished. No longer did I care that the Latvians were copying six of my best selling items and serving the same brand of coffee that I advertised. I felt forgiveness for the mysterious Institute. I felt a sense of pride and deep friendship for the new bookstore and its owners. I fell in love with the magnificent building and all its private places even more than I had before.

The guests began to laugh and bump into one another. As they reached for the small repast, I looked up to see Barry's shadow in the upstairs recess. He had been watching from above, apart from all of us. And then he left without a word.

Chapter 36

WITH THE SAME INTENSITY that I started to construct my Sedona coffee shop and food adventure, I began the next step: to position my jewel for sale. I made an appointment with the best commercial real estate broker in Sedona.

He was a cool customer, a devilishly handsome Italian who had an office that was dripping with the masculine trappings of red leather. The décor emanated power and was filled with polished brass, heavy wood and Renaissance statues. He was the broker I had called many months earlier in regard to the personal guarantee. Santino Carlucchi had style, confidence, and an ultra-smooth manner. He had done some of the biggest deals in town and sat on a larded back account. Counting on the ever-optimistic new upstarts and merchants who were retiring, expanding or selling out, Santino's services were always in demand. The office had a designer look and smelled like a mixture of French vetivert perfume and Cuban cigar smoke. Both aromas advertised money and clung to Santino. Deep blue hydrangeas blossoms reminded me of cotton candy spun around popcorn balls and stood two feet tall in an exquisite heavy, cut crystal vase. The edges of the vase reflected rainbows. The zebra wood humidor had a deep shine of patina that reflected my face as I sat down. I wanted to peek inside for a look at the tobacco collection.

As I presented my case, he gave me comment after comment, point-by-point, of the shaky market. Undaunted, I asked him questions about his service and fee. Santino had been to my coffee shop many times, since it was a perfect hunting ground on his safari for business deals. Many of his would-be clients had lunched there on his tab. His office was a brisk ten-minute walk from the coffee shop and he knew the history of the former businesses in the building, from the multi-million dollar movie theatre owner to the other start-ups who had tried and failed.

Now he sat back in his high backed, executive throne and royally granted me permission to plead my case. I based my interest in a sale due to the impending surgery to my hand that my physician had warned me about. I didn't bother to mention chest pains, sleepless nights and an elevated blood pressure. I did not talk about the deep splits on my fingertips. We discussed the landlord bringing in a similar concept next door and how the Latvians could not exist selling sprats, herring, and beet salad. Granted they had European groceries: chocolates and canned goods in their small market, but what was the market for forest mushrooms, Polish sausage, and elderberry juice in Northern Arizona? Their deli was a parallel business to mine and I felt the eyes of a peregrine falcon spying on my sales daily as they copied my best selling soups and sandwiches.

Santino just seemed amused by my account and assured me he knew what my predicament was. He asked me what dollar value I would place on the business and what figures Mr. Sterling had given me at the year's end. When I told him we had grossed over $120 thousand in sales against $115 thousand in expenses, he looked at me in disbelief. When he asked me what figure I had in mind to sell, he laughed in my face. I left the meeting stung by his rudeness; his condescension negating any possibility for a deal and stinging like the desert plant, the Spanish dagger, whose barbs slice your legs when you pass by too closely.

A week later, Santino called to say he had a very young client who needed a taco shop and could offer $25 thousand. I had not signed any agreement and the call left me cold and angry over the rudeness of another bloody lash.

Jimmy was home for a few days, resting from jetting all around the country and offered an option: the Internet had businesses for sale and would reach a national market. The fees were much lower, a mere $150 to list an advertisement instead of a whopping twenty percent of the selling price that Santino had quoted.

As Jimmy helped me place the advertisement with facts and photos, I prepared a handout for the serious future seekers. Naturally, it was enveloped in a grape colored folder. I placed our glistening gold seal, complete with the unclothed figures flying through space being dragged by the anterior portion of a horse, onto the cover. Sometimes, I imagined I was that woman, balanced precariously on a man's hand.

My instructions were clear in the take-home package that contained a one-page story, the facts, the inventory and crucial figures. "Just like a house you decide to buy, make an offer. If it is accepted, proceed to the Sedona Title Company at the address listed on the last page and deposit your earnest money with Littlestar Hadley, Title Officer," the folder instructed.

In the first thirty days following the *Puja*, I received twenty-two inquiries and mailed that number of folders. Between Barry and me, we conducted six personal tours of the café. Prospective buyers carried a packet home.

A new feeling of peacefulness crept in and sat next to a loss of personality and emotions in both Barry and me. It was a feeling of resignation and acceptance. A sense of limbo and sadness laced the edges of the mourning cloth.

Since Barry couldn't keep a secret about anything, I had to swear the loose-lipped talker to silence. As far as our expressions were concerned, we were both flatter than a Sunday morning pancake at a church breakfast.

Chapter 37

THE CLINIC WAS BUSIER than usual. Along with two other techs, I watched as the medical chopper lifted off, taking the badly injured patient we had just X-rayed down to Barrows in Phoenix.

My cell phone buzzed with the light flashing. Since I had a free moment, I answered it.

"Reesie-Baby, you'll never believe this! Some guy has been in here for about a half hour now. He needs to talk to you. He wants to buy the café!" Barry was panting.

"Book him. Book him tomorrow at five, I'll talk to him as soon as I'm through," I said.

"Why not today, when you're finished?" Barry asked.

"Let him marinate a little and let me get my thoughts organized. See ya."

"Okay, you're the boss, Butter Lump."

I wasn't really as excited as Barry. He clearly wanted out and to take an easy stress-less job in Sedona. He had been pointing out that we both actually could have a great life in Sedona and live instead of slave here. He presented a case for going to the art shows, the fairs, the Sedona Film Festival and the Jazz on the Rocks annual concert. We could have friends outside of the café, have people over for dinner, give small parties, take weekend trips and do all the things others got to do here in the rockery wonderland.

For me, something was going to be missing. I had put so much of my personal selections into creating the café. I put my heart into it. *There is no loss or grief in the World, only opportunities*, says the Buddha. The numbness that was now my only emotion scared me a little. The entirety of the adventure had left me so flat; I felt like a walking zombie just showing up and going through the repeat motions everyday. And Barry wasn't funny anymore, no matter how hard he tried.

I met with Daniel the next day, promptly at five. We sat outside on the patio because I needed to have some privacy in our discussions. I was keeping all news of the sale of the café a secret from the town, the neighbors, the landlord, and the crew. I didn't want complications and I was a big enough girl to know the deal wasn't a 'done deal' until I could feel a real check in my hands, smell the cash, and see the gray-green money on the barrelhead.

Daniel was frighteningly thin and showed up carrying

one of the crafty purple folders I had prepared. I noticed he had a navy blue checkbook on top of the Weathervane Café folder.

"So Dan, did you take a tour of the property yesterday?" I asked. "Did you see the storage room, my office, and all the equipment?"

"Yup, Barry showed me everything, even some photos of the before and after. It's a nice transformation."

"So, what are you looking for Dan?" Funny, how I was in the seller's position wearing a different hat in the opposite seat.

"May I call you, Resa?"

"Sure."

"Well, a little about Judy and me. We own a house here. We've been wintering here from California for fifteen years now. We love Sedona."

"Who doesn't? I chuckled.

The Californians were streaming in droves to Arizona after wildfires, floods, earthquakes, and the rise in housing prices. They had cash and a lot of it from selling their 1600 square foot homes for a half a million dollars. Then they would turn around and buy up choice Arizona properties sight unseen. This guy wanted a business to keep Judy busy and to flush money into a five-year, income tax-averaging option on his 1040 to the Feds.

"I've already done my homework on every available space up for sale here in Sedona and this definitely fits what we want. The parking's great. It's beautiful." Dan wasted no time.

"So what I'm hearing is that you don't want the coffee shop or the name or the concept. You just want the space?" I asked, clarifying the conversation. Dan nodded.

"Judy and I started with a small organic market. We turned that over and over until we had done that three times."

"I see." We were sipping some nice drink selections: a hot chai latte for Dan and pink lemonade over ice for me.

"Judy's a vegan like me, too, and a great cook. So we started an all-vegetarian café next to the market. That was another winner. Now we're here full time. We sold out of California completely."

"What's your vision here, Dan?"

"We want to bring in our California artists that we've used before, their graphics, their style, and choice of colors, you know."

I nodded, listening.

"We're going to duplicate our last business, our vegan concept: a raw food and organic restaurant here in Sedona. The Town's ripe for it. Gonna call it the 'Golden Carrot' and I'm ready right now to make you an offer." He fingered his checkbook. Then he added, "I want possession in six weeks." He had just sweetened the pot!

It was lucky that my emotions had taken a holiday without me and I was so deadpan. That *Puja* really did work wonders.

Dan was on his game. "I'm ready to offer you $80 thousand right here and now, CASH," he stated. His eyes were drilling holes into mine and we were playing poker now at a green felt table at Binion's World Wide Championship Play-Offs. There were high stakes, bluffs, raises, and holds on the table.

"That's not what I had in mind, Dan, with all the improvements, the new equipment, the track record, the clientele, the retail space, why, you're low, way low."

"But your figure's indicate you only grossed $120K last year; you're not making any money," he came on strong.

"Yes, but we can make a lot more money with evening hours, liquor, dinners, and the wedding trade. We get a lot of business from the nearby resorts. We're poised to move up twenty percent this coming season. And, Dan, all that I've spent on advertising it's going to help the new owner. People are used to coming here for the great coffee."

"I'll up my offer to $90K. I'll write the check right now," he countered.

"My price is $140K. Check your folder. And I have a phone call to make. I have a silent partner that I will need to talk to about this meeting. Right now we're too far apart, but I will welcome a counter offer." I raised my hand in a warning gesture to keep him from opening the checkbook. "Why don't you talk to Judy? I'd love to meet her and let's get together tomorrow, same time. Over night think about what you can do, Dan—there's a lot of heart and soul in this business and don't forget, you're offering to buy my good will. That comes at a little higher price."

Dan's eyes fell and focused on the navy blue checkbook. He was thinking through the logic of all I was saying. I was expressionless and as cold as ice. He hadn't expected

257

some business-wise answers and a delay to his cash offer.

Barry was pacing up and down when I entered the café. He wanted a quick, sure sale at any price and he was literally tap dancing with nerves.

"Well?"

'That's a deep subject."

"Well what?"

"We're fifty thousand apart," I told him.

"You mean he made an offer?"

"Yeah, one that pays the bank off and gives you a back salary and nothing to me for all my investment or any compensation for my hard work."

"Resa, I can't believe you didn't take it," he was flustered.

"Believe it, Barry. He'll be back for the plum," I said, as I walked stoic-like to the back room.

I walked all through the café: the retail alcove, the mop room, and my under-stairway pantry that felt so cozy. Seeing all the industrial-sized cans and case lots of goods made me feel a sense of plenty. Maybe the Mormons felt the same way when they checked their year's supply of groceries hidden away for the catastrophe. I ambled to the office where the gift baskets were assembled and the financial records were kept. The feeling that was playing in my heart, right then and there, was a song of farewell.

When I pulled myself together, I started an order of napalitos salad. After all, there would be at least six more weeks of bills to pay and rent would actually be due two more times. As he passed, I whispered to Barry, "Come by later tonight, we'll talk then." For once, he was speechless. He gave me a long grim look.

♦♦♦♦♦♦♦♦♦♦

It was after sunset when Barry arrived at my Sedona-home, as I called my bungalow. "Let's head out and take a walk," I suggested.

We were both subdued, trudging along in silence, picking up the evening smells of juniper, hackberry and ironwood. The Gambol quail scattered about and were bedding down and hiccoughing their last "kwerk, kwerk, kwerks" of the day. The prickly pears around the neighborhood were growing fatter, still just pink-tinged, green spheres promising a harvest of fall fruit. *The Buddha maintains that in silence we get close to our inner self, to the Knowing.*

"So what are you going to do, Resa?" Barry asked in a sweet, gentle voice.

"Dan's positioned to bite. We just need to come to terms," I answered back. "He really wants the spot. The *Golden Carrot*, can you imagine?" It caught in my throat like a rasp and the tears jumped from my eyes.

The stars were putting on their coming-out party. They were little white-gowned debutantes, all glittery in diamonds and pearls.

"Sure is a gorgeous evening…" he murmured. I was concentrating, deep in swirling thoughts.

"You need to be the go-between, Barry. You need to

plant the seed; he's got the sale if he splits the difference. You know what to say. I'll close at $120 thousand."

"The suggestion will be delivered tomorrow, my dear."

"You've been right all along. It was a massive undertaking," I admitted.

"Are you going to miss it? Are you going to be okay with the sale?" The old psychologist was probing my feelings.

"It's been a wild rodeo ride for this cowgirl, but, you know, Barry, what a great experience," I mused.

"You had some kind of courage…"

"Or just plain stupidity!" We laughed a little.

"Reese," he said quietly, "Are you going miss the coffee shop and all you did there?"

His question brought more hot salty tears to my eyes.

By this time we were walking hand in hand. I looked up at the God-given swath of millions of white, lucky-stone stars that pave a grand Milky Way, so bright and wide that the staircase to Heaven takes up most of the night sky. One cannot stand under that pathway of shimmering luster and be unimpressed. I turned to Barry.

"I'll always have this, my Sedona, this place here in my heart under all these stars."

Chapter 38

DAN AND JUDY CAME by the next day as planned. I gave them a little extra time by hanging back at the clinic to give them some space for another look at the equipment, to fall in love a little deeper, and to give Barry some time to speak "man to man" to Dan.

Judy was ultra-scrawny. Next to her I felt a head taller and a cow pony's weight heavier.

The four of us stood in the non-kitchen while their eyes were taking mental measurements for their future overhaul. Dan led off.

"Judy and I have put our heads together and are willing to go up to $120K," announced Dan.

"Then it's a done deal," I answered as we all smiled and shook hands.

There were pleasant proper smiles of acknowledgement and the slight nods that registered agreement and congratulations. The four of us were acting very dignified. Barry, the convincing non-stop talker, had played the part of a slick sideshow barker and Dan had made up his mind long ago to get this space, one of the classiest in the West End of town.

Instead of relief or joy or even excitement, the feeling that I identified, as the small talk went on, was numb detachment. I was outside myself, listening to the others converse as I observed the scene from a distance away.

"And here's where the new gas grill will be installed," said Dan happily, as he gestured to the center of the worktables. My eyebrows raised a little at the mental calculations of the cost of installation. "We'll lower it to make it comfortable for Judy," he continued. "We'll be adding another large refrigerator and the alcove will become my office. We won't need the retail inventory," Dan went on.

Barry and I exchanged a look. I could tell he wanted to argue about the proposed changes we were hearing. It was Judy's turn and she began by relating her future menu.

"We plan to offer vege-burgers, tofurkey, tempeh, quorn, seitan, and date shakes. They're very popular," she said.

Barry's look to me said 'blahh,' but his thoughts turned back to coffee.

"You'll find the espresso machines easy to use. By noon they generate about a-buck to a-buck-and-a-half in change. It's your bread and butter and the rent money," he said.

Dan piped up, "We're taking the espresso machines out. We're not serving coffee."

My gaze registered surprise and resignation as my heart sunk and I shot a look at Barry to keep quiet.

"Vegans don't drink coffee," added Judy. "We'll serve Postum or chicory. I like a blend that has roasted grains, persimmon seeds, sweet potato peels, and beet root.

"Ahaaa," I said, with eyes wide open as my stomach turned a little.

"Our colors will be in line with earth tones and we're going to use our former designer from our last business," Dan stated. He opened a folder and displayed color swatches of baby-poop, yellow-brown and a flashy gilded sign with their California logo: *The Golden Carrot*.

A sinking feeling grabbed my gut over the loss of the beautiful look that has spruced up the coffee shop. The huge new sense of loss was arriving like a roaring freight train.

"Also, the landlord is allowing us to take the two big trees down on each side of the patio," Judy added.

I felt my lips pursing into a pucker and I rolled my eyes to the corners of the ceiling to keep from spouting unwanted advice.

"You might want to rethink that when the summer heat gets here. You will need the shade because of the high windows," said Barry.

"No, they're coming out," countered Judy.

We all got quiet for a moment since the conversation was becoming uncomfortable.

We were still standing, circle-like, when a small mouse ran across the space between the four of us. Right before our eyes the little critter committed suicide—it ran directly into a trap peeking out beneath the counter. We all froze. My first fearful thought was that the sale would now become null and void. Dan and Judy seemed non-pulsed.

"Gotcha!" Barry whooped.

I took it as a sign.

Chapter 39

THE NEW OWNERS PROVED true to their word and were serious in their dealings with the purchase. They were as good as gold. Dan was an ultra -sharp businessman and a certified real estate attorney licensed in California. Therefore, he was able to both negotiate with Stein and command respect from him as a future tenant.

The announcement of the sale was made two weeks prior to the takeover to prepare the staff for the inevitable change and also to give them notice. So the firing of Grant never took place. Dan and Judy had the pick of the litter and, alas, since they took several months to install a state of the art kitchen, my staff looked elsewhere for employment. They needed a weekly paycheck, not a hiatus of income.

To soften the blow, I planned a lasagna dinner

complete with red jug wine and a big salad for the crew. It was out of a sense of gratitude and to continue the feeling of family we had fostered. Barry didn't try to stop me, but commented that, "I was a pushover, again."

During that last week of official ownership, either Barry or I would stop by the table of a regular customer and share a few words. Some of our ladies would see me again at the clinic. For some others, we would pass at the movies or in the local grocery store. They had been loyal customers to us.

As far as the Intergalactic Space Travelers group, they were the most uplifting and made a philosophic statement regarding the upcoming change in ownership

"The Universe has a cycle and a balance. Change is constant...and an all vegan restaurant would be perfect!" Their observations made me feel so much better.

The Business Brainstormers would continue coming and hold their meeting at their usual table.

When I started getting phone calls at home, voices begging to know the ingredients in the chicken sandwich or the prickly pear salad dressing—one patron wanted it served in a soup bowl – I knew another job was in my future: to share the tastes with my larger audience.

That last day, just before the appointment at the Sedona Title Company, when official ownership would be transferred to Dan and Judy, I was packing a few of my personal things. I didn't want to forget Grandpa's blue-steel filet knife. It had been my mainstay as well as my Cuisinart food processor. With my head in a packing box,

I heard the cultured voice that had been a solace during the past year. Roland had provided thoughts of culinary delights from time to time and he jolted me back to the reality of this ending.

"Resa, I just heard, you're leaving?"

He looked at me with those yearning eyes. I felt guilty at having forgotten to make a special effort to call him personally.

"Oh, Roland, it's for the best. I just can't maintain." I tried to make a little joke by blaming my age: double nickels, the sunny side of sixty.

"There is something here that the new vegans don't want in the inventory. They can't use…I want you to have it, Roland. No one else would appreciate it. I want you to remember me."

I reached for the boxed caviar bowl on my retail shelf. It had a serving bowl for ice and two hand-carved horn spoons which accompanied the set. Never taking his eyes from mine, as the box passed from my hands to his, Roland accepted the gift. We stood there for a silent moment and then he turned and left.

Chapter 40

SINCE THE SALE SIX months earlier, I hadn't seen Barry after he left town. His invitation was a nice surprise. He was entrenched in another chapter in his career calling on some old experience in investigation and had settled into a condo with a view of the Las Vegas Strip. We had exchanged a few e-mails to keep up with the major and minor changes since we left the café. He had gotten back into the family fold after telling his tale of success as the general manager of the café.

"So what will it be for the evening, my little Turtle Dove?" he asked as he opened his door.

"Oh, the usual, Barry, a great classic meal, the right music ,and a quiet velvet draped alcove."

"I know just the place."

The view from the open French doors gave a long sight line of the Rio and the Stratosphere in the distance. We were relaxed, enjoying the moment. Barry was puttering with his electric LaRoma espresso machine. He was a mad scientist with the distilled water, the Italian coffee grounds and the tamping.

"What do you plan for your next project, Resa? I know how you are, always busy," he asked.

"Some time to relax, a trip somewhere. Then an announcement for the Sedona wedding of Lacey and Jimmy," I replied. "And you, Barry?"

"There's a fresh sleuth mission I'll be undertaking. A chapter of Dick Tracy adventure ahead for me," he shared.

He served us a smooth espresso in white porcelain cups. We toasted one another.

"Well, we had the best when it came to coffee, didn't we?"

"Sure did. What did the doctor say about the tingly heart pains?" he asked.

"I'll have to find a decaf that's drinkable."

Then he handed me a gift-wrapped box.

"Remember the lights of Jerome on the forehead of the night?" he asked. Inside was a rhinestone tiara.

"Then that's my goal, my dear, to stalk that rare bean. There's a naturally grown un-caffeinated variety, the Mascarocaffe Vianney. It exists somewhere in the wilds of Madagascar."

PostMortem

THE BRAINSTORMERS STILL GET together on the patio of the new vegan palace, the *Golden Carrot*. Their chosen project is for a series of dollhouses for children of all religious and spiritual followings. Their plans include a small Hindu temple, imprinted with miniature monks and nuns in orange robes, a Buddhist monastery, Roman cathedrals, with a parade of cardinals and the Pope, French convents with tiny nuns, a Judea temple featuring a small cantor and rabbi, a replica of the Sikhs Golden Temple in Amritsar, and an Arab mosque with colorful prayer rugs. The temples, mosques, and churches will be equipped with the piped-in sounds of chanting and hymns. Incense, smoke and gold leaf are included in the deluxe editions. Customized versions are made to order. I want a replica of the Castle Church in Wittenberg where Luther nailed his ninety-five theses. Lacey is asking for a Santa Fe mission. Sissy has ordered a replica of the cathedral at Charters. The sales are projected to be astronomical and children will learn about different faiths as they play with the tiny figures and ecclesiastic architecture. Barry has sent a Hebrew temple to his mother who was thrilled at the thought. He's back in her good graces.

Dipti and Ranjit call themselves Betty and George again. She has moved back to the Valley of the Sun after paying off the $300 citation for feeding wildlife. George takes care of maintenance at a Sedona resort and lives on the premises. He's dating again.

The Filipino boys have new jobs. Sweet young Grant works with special needs children in Cottonwood. Gerry drives an evening taxi in town and Gordon does his tattoos full-time up on the mountain in Jerome.

Bobby Begay and Flint Painted Horse saved the town with Bobby's marshmallow shooter. It took them all night to lure the critters at a slow walk back to where they belonged behind the Aerie, and the City of Sedona gave them a ceremony of thanks and commendation held at the Library.

The new vegan restaurant is busy and doing well. They even got a spot on *Bizarre Foods* on the *Food Channel*. The Inter-Galactic Space Travelers group still meets on the patio. There hasn't been an actual visitation or an alien abduction; however, they are hopefully waiting.

The Lutheran church accepted nine boxes of coffee cups from the café with the nude figures on them. The Sprout Kid sells his assortment at the big organic market, New Foods.

Lacey and Jimmy have set a date: a wedding at the Church of the Red Rocks, a reception above Oak Creek in the old Bacon Rind Park at Indian Gardens followed by a honeymoon in Las Vegas.

The Latvians next door serve coffee, but it's not as good as ours.

Coffee Recipes

Café Mocha

2 to 3 shots espresso
¾ cup steamed milk
2 oz chocolate syrup
Sugar to taste
Whipped cream or foamed milk
Chocolate curls

Café Almond Latte

2 shots espresso
2 oz almond syrup
2 TBS sweetened condensed milk
¾ cup steamed milk
Whipped cream
Almond slices

Caramel Macchiato

3 shots cold espresso
¾ cup cold milk
3 oz caramel syrup
½ cup ice
Blend till smooth
Whipped cream and a drizzle
Of caramel syrup

The Rummy

2 shots cold espresso
½ cup ice
2 TBS sweetened condensed milk
½ cup cold milk
3 oz rum syrup
Shake well, top with whipped cream
Sprinkle with ground cloves

Vanilla Latte

2 to 3 shots espresso
3 oz vanilla syrup
¾ cup milk
2 TBS sweetened condensed milk
Foamed milk
Sprinkles of Vanilla Sugar

Cinnamon Latte

3 shots espresso
2 oz cinnamon syrup
1 TBS light brown sugar
¾ cup steamed milk
Foamed milk
Whipped cream
Stick cinnamon and a dusting of ground cinnamon.

The Viennese

3 shots espresso
¾ cup steamed milk
2 TBS sweetened condensed milk
1/8 tsp each, ground cinnamon, ground cloves, ground nutmeg
Whipped cream
Dusting of spices on top

The Orange Blossom

2 shots espresso
2 oz orange syrup
1 oz brandy syrup
¾ cup steamed milk
Whipped cream
Candied orange peel

Almond Joy

3 shots espresso
¾ cup steamed milk
1 oz almond syrup
1 oz coconut syrup
1 oz chocolate syrup
Whipped cream
Coconut flakes
Drizzle of chocolate syrup

The Hazelnut Latte

2 shots of espresso
¾ cup steamed milk
2 oz hazelnut syrup
Whipped cream
A dusting of ground hazelnuts
Drizzle of chocolate syrup

Gingerbread Latte

2 shots of espresso
1/2 cup steamed milk
½ cup brewed coffee
3 oz gingerbread syrup
Whipped cream
Dusting of spices
Maraschino cherry

Peppermint Patty

2 shots espresso
½ cup steamed milk
½ cup brewed coffee
1 oz cream de menthe syrup
2 oz chocolate syrup
Whipped cream
Drizzle of green cream de menthe syrup
Chocolate stick

White Chocolate Latte

3 shots espresso
¾ cup steamed milk
3 oz white chocolate syrup
Whipped cream
Chocolate sprinkles

Arabian Night

3 oz espresso
½ cup brewed coffee
1 tsp ground cardamom
2 TBS sweetened condensed milk
½ cup steamed milk
Top with foamed milk
Dust with ground cardamom

Recipes from the

Weathervane Café

APPETIZERS

COWBOY CAVIAR
8oz cream cheese
8oz jar dried shredded beef, rinsed
1 finely minced green onion
1 tbsp. minced red pepper
1 tbsp. caper berries, rinsed and dried
Dash of ground black pepper

Mix cream cheese until smooth, add all other ingredients with a folding action until blended. Serve on crackers or pita triangles and garnish plate with greens and thinly sliced radishes.

NAPALITO WITH GOAT CHEESE/JALAPINO DRESSING

This is a recipe that calls for fresh napalitos pads, not the jarred version. The little extra work makes for a superior finished dish.

½ lb fresh Napalitos pads
Batter:
1 c buttermilk
½ c flour
½ c finely ground blue cornmeal
1 tsp. salt
1 tsp. baking powder
½ c corn starch
1 egg white
1 tbsp. Hatch red chili powder finely ground
Peanut oil for deep frying

De-thorn, peel, and cut into 2"x1/2" strips the fresh napalito pads and blanch in boiling water for 1 minute. Drain on paper towels. Dip in batter, fry until golden in 360 degree peanut oil, drain on paper towels. To serve, drizzle with Goat Cheese Jalapino Dressing and dust with a little red chili powder.

GOAT CHEESE JALAPINO DRESSING
    4 oz. goat cheese
    1 fresh small jalapino, seeded and minced
    dash black pepper
    ½ tsp. Hatch Red Chili Powder
    ¼ tsp. salt
    ¼ tsp. lemon zest
    1 c buttermilk

Combine all ingredients in food processor and mix until creamy.

QUESO QUESADILLA WITH MANGO SALSA
    2 large flour tortillas
    ½ c shredded Bear Flag Monterey Jack Cheese

Place cheese on ½ of tortilla, fold other half to cover and grill until lightly brown and cheese is melted. Flip once. Repeat with second tortilla. Cut into wedges. Serve garnished with fresh cilantro leaves and a ramekin of Mango Salsa.

MANGO SALSA

1 1/2c fresh or frozen mango, coarsely chopped

2 tbsp. purple onion, minced

½ c fresh tomato, peeled, seeded and cut in 1/4" pieces

1 small jalapino, seeded and minced

1 tbsp. fresh parsley, minced

2 tbsp. small capers, drained

2 tbsp. cilantro leaves

¼ c fresh lime juice

1 tbsp. lime zest

½ tsp. salt

Stir ingredients until well blended. Refrigerate.

BLACK BEAN CAKES WITH CILANTRO LIME SAUCE

15 oz can Black Beans drained

½ c frozen yellow corn

4 tbsp. purple onion

4 tbsp. fresh cilantro

1 tbsp. celery leaves

1 tbsp. fresh parsley

½ c whole wheat flour (or substitute matzos meal, all purpose flour, or fine ground corn

meal)

1 tsp. salt

½ tsp. cumin

1 tsp. Hatch Red Chili Powder (or a minced Pasillio green chili)

1 tbsp. corn oil

1 egg , lightly beaten

½ c cotija cheese crumbled

Coating:

½ c all purpose flour

¼ c cornmeal

1 tbsp. Hatch Red Chili Powder

Mix ingredients and set aside.

In food processor, chop onion, cilantro, celery leaves, parsley, with dry ingredients. Add beans and pulse 1-3 times, leaving beans coarse. Transfer to mixing bowl, add egg, cheese and corn and mix until blended. Refrigerate for 1 hour or more. Mixture should be stiff enough to form hamburger sized patties (add more flour or cornmeal if mixture is too soft.) Dip both sides of pattie in coating and fry in a non-stick skillet until brown on both sides. Serve cakes on hot platter topped with a dollop of Red Chili Mayonnaise and a ramekin of Cilantro Lime Sauce on side for dipping.

CILANTRO LIME SAUCE

    ½ c raw baby spinach leaves
    1c packed fresh cilantro
    ½ c vegetable oil
    ¼ c olive oil
    1/3 c lime juice
    1 packet Four Seasons Salad Dressing mix
    1 tbsp. lime zest

Puree all ingredients, salt and pepper to taste.

MIXED FIELD GREEN SALAD

  2 c mixed field greens, washed, dried, and chilled
  1 tbsp. purple onion, thinly sliced
  2 radishes, thinly sliced
  10-12 pieces jicama, julienned in ¼"x2" matchsticks
  4 cherry tomatoes, halved
  ½ avocado sliced, dipped in fresh lemon or lime juice
  1/8 red, yellow, or purple pepper, chopped

Arrange vegetables on bed of greens. Serve with dressing of choice.

CREAM OF PARSLEY DRESSING

    2 cloves fresh garlic
    1 c packed parsley
    1 c vegetable oil
    ½ c olive oil
    ½ c fresh lemon juice
    1 tbsp. lemon zest
    1 tsp. salt
    ½ tsp. pepper
    1 tbsp. Dijon mustard, or 1 tsp. dried mustard

Puree ingredients in blender until creamy.

JICAMA SALAD

1 medium jicama, peeled until white flesh is visible, remove any brown flecks and cut or

julienne on mandoline into ¼"x2" matchstick pieces, toss with 1/2c lime juice

1 c cooked or canned shoe peg corn

1 c celery, finely chopped

¼ c purple onion, cut in thin matchsticks

1 red pepper, seeded and chopped in ½" pieces

2 tbsp. parsley, chopped

4 tbsp. cilantro leaves, stems removed and chopped

1 ½ tsp. salt

1 tbsp. lime zest

½ c olive oil

½ c vegetable oil

Toss all ingredients with jicama, chill 30 minutes and serve on cold plates drizzled with Cilantro Lime Dressing.

BLACK BEAN SALAD

16 oz cooked black beans, or canned and drained black beans

2 stalks celery hearts, chopped

4 tbsp. purple onion, minced

½ red pepper, chopped

1 large tomato, chopped

4 oz. yellow or white corn, cooked or clanned

1 tbsp. parsley, chopped

2 tbsp. cilantro leaves, chopped

2 tbsp. cojita cheese, crumbled

Toss all ingredients, chill. Serve on a chilled plate of greens, drizzle with Cilantro Lime Dressing.

CAVE CREEK TROUT SALAD

1 lb. grilled, cubed and chilled trout, cut into 1" squares

1 tbsp. purple onion, minced

½ c celery, sliced

¼ c red pepper, cut into ¼" pieces

½ c Green Mayonnaise

1 tbsp. Hatch Mild Red Chili Powder

Toss all ingredients, chill. Serve on a chilled plate of greens. Garnish with 4 cherry tomatoes, halved, drizzle with Cilantro Lime Dressing, and top with thin, fried corn chips. (Fresh Catfish, tuna or halibut may be substituted for trout.)

GREEN MAYONNAISE
1c Basic Mayonnaise
2 or 3 drops Boyajian Lime Oil
1 tsp. lime zest
1 tbsp. Hatch Green Chili Powder
4 tbsp. cilantro leaves
2 tbsp. baby spinach leaves

In blender, puree lime oil, zest, chili powder, cilantro leaves and spinach leaves until smooth. Add Basic Mayonnaise and mix until blended. Refrigerate and use within 5 days.

ZUNI SPINACH SALAD
    2 c baby spinach leaves, washed and spun dry
    4-6 fresh strawberries, sliced vertically to reveal heart
shape
    2 tbsp. dried cranberries
    2 tbsp. chopped pecan
    8-10 matchstick sized pieces of purple onion

    Toss gently with Prickly Pear Dressing on chilled
plates.

PRICKLEY PEAR DRESSING
 1 packet Four Seasons Italian Salad Dressing
 ½ c Prickley Pear Jelly
 1/c vegetable oil
 ¼ c white wine vinegar
 ¼ c sugar or honey
 1 tbsp. poppy seeds
 ¼ c water

Puree all ingredients, except poppy seeds, in blender until smooth. Stir in poppy seeds and refrigerate.

NAPALITOS SALAD
 3 c mixed greens or torn romaine leaves
 1 ½ c napalitos strips, rinsed and drained
 2 tbsp. purple onion, cut into 1" matchsticks
 1 avocado, cubed
 1 large tomato, peeled, seeded and cubed
 ¼ c fresh cilantro leaves, whole
 ¼ c cojita cheese, crumbled

Layer greens on chilled platter, scatter napalitos strips evenly on top. Layer remaining ingredients, ending with cheese on top. Drizzle with dressing and garnish with additional cilantro leaves.

 Dressing:
 2 cloves garlic, minced
 2-3 drops Boyajian Lime Oil
 1/3 c fresh lime juice
 ¾ c olive oil (or a mixture of olive and vegetable oil)
 1 tsp. salt
 ½ tsp. black pepper

Blend all ingredients until smooth.

SONORAN CHICKEN SANDWICH WITH RED CHILI
MAYONNAISE
4 oz. chicken breast filet, mesquite grilled
Leaf lettuce
Tomato slices
Purple onion slices
Fresh sprouts
Toasted Sourdough bread or large tortilla grilled, but
pliable
Red Chili Mayonnaise

Serve as a sandwich or wrap.

RED CHILI MAYONNAISE

    1 c Basic Mayonnaise

    ¼ c Sriracha Hot Chili Sauce*

    Stir in chili sauce to taste. Refrigerate, use within 5 days.

    *Sriracha Hot Chili Sauce can be purchased from Huy Fong Foods, Inc., 5001 Earle Ave., Rosemead, CA 91770-1169, Tel. 626-286-8328, www.huyfong.com

CHAPARRAL HAM SANDWICH WITH SAGE MUSTARD

    2 slices rye bread, or Kaiser roll grilled
    3 slices baked ham
    1 slice Bear Flag Monterey Jack Cheese
    Baby spinach leaves
    Sliced tomato
    Sage Mustard

Serve sandwich with a side salad and dill pickle.

SAGE MUSTARD

    1 c Basic Mayonnaise

    1/3 c Dijon Mustard

    8-10 fresh sage leaves, pounded in a mortar to a paste with ½ tsp. salt and ½ tsp. pepper

    Mix together mayonnaise and mustard until smooth. Add pounded sage leaves and blend until smooth. Refrigerate.

BASIC MAYONNAISE
   1 large egg, plus 3 large egg yolks
   2 tbsp. fresh lemon juice or distilled white vinegar
   ¼ tsp. salt
   ¼ tsp. white pepper
   ½ tsp. dry mustard
   1 ¼ vegetable oil at room temperature

In food processor, add all ingredients, except oil, and blend until smooth. Drizzle oil in thin stream until mixture thickens. Refrigerate.

DIABLO ROAST BEEF WITH GREEN HORSERADISH

2 slices sourdough bread or Kaiser Roll or Large Tortilla Wrap

3 slices rare roast beef, thinly sliced

1 slice swiss cheese

Leaf lettuce

1 slice purple onion, thin

2 slices tomato

Pickle

Arrange in sandwich, spread bread or wrap with Green Horseradish. Serve with pickle on side.

GREEN HORSERADISH

1 c Basic Mayonnaise

2 tbsp. Wasabi Paste or Powder

2 tbsp. fresh grated, peeled horseradish

Mix ingredients and refrigerate until ready to use.

GREEN CHILI PORK POSOLE

¼ c. vegetable oil

3 lbs. cubed pork shoulder

6 cloves garlic, minced

1 ½ c yellow onion, cubed small

4 stalks celery, sliced ½"

1 large carrot, sliced

32 oz. can hominy corn, drained, rinsed

15 oz. can diced tomatoes or 3 large fresh tomatoes, diced

2 large potatoes, cubed ½" or 2/3 c potato flakes

2-3 bay leaves

2 tsp. salt

1 tsp. black pepper

2 c. Mild Hatch Green Chilies, diced, fresh or frozen or 4-6 tbsp. green chili powder

1 red pepper, seeded and cut in ½" pieces

¼ c. fresh cilantro, chopped

¼ c. fresh parsley, minced

Brown pork cubes on all sides in oil. Add garlic, onion, celery, carrot, sauté 5-10 minutes. Add hominy and enough water to cover, simmer covered 1 ½ hours. Stir occasionally and add more water or stock if needed. Add all other ingredients and simmer covered 1 hour longer. The liquid should be slightly thickened when done.

Season to taste. Serve with corn chips and fresh cilantro sprigs.

CACTUS RED CHILI BEEF
  5 lbs. beef brisket
  ¼ c. vegetable oil
  4 cloves garlic, coarsely chopped
  2 large yellow onions, chopped
  1 large carrot, shredded
  ½ c. Mild Hatch Red Chili Powder
  ½ c. fresh celery leaves, chopped
  2 c. tomato juice
  1 c. water or stock
  2 tsp. salt
  1 tsp. black pepper
  ½ c. flour mixed in 3/4c water
  16 oz. jar Napalitos, rinsed and drained

Brown brisket in vegetable oil. Add garlic, onions, carrot, celery leaves and chili powder to oil and sauté until vegetables are soft and chili powder is toasted, but not burned. Add tomato juice, water, and seasonings and simmer covered for 4 hours until beef shreds easily with a fork. Add napalitos and flour mixture to shredded beef, mix to combine and simmer 30 minutes more. Beef should have a gravy-like sauce. To serve, heat a large tortilla, add a layer of beef, top with chopped raw tomato, shredded lettuce, grated cheese, minced raw onion and roll up burrito-style.

PRICKLEY PEAR LEMONADE
    1 quart sugar
    1 gallon water
    8-10 lemon rinds
    juice of 8-10 lemons, reserved
    ½ c. Cheris Prickly Pear Syrup

Boil lemon rinds with 1 quart of water for 8-10 minutes in a non-reactive pan. Strain. Add sugar to hot liquid, stir and cool. Add remaining water, lemon juice and syrup to create a deep blush color with the distinctive (background) flavor of the Prickly Pear Syrup. Serve over ice, garnished with fresh mint leaves.

OAK CREEK CANYON TROUT WITH PECAN AND JUNIPER BERRY BUTTER SAUCE

2 ½ lbs. fresh trout filets
1 tbsp. grapeseed oil
¼ c. pecans, crushed
4 tbsp. melted butter
12 juniper berries, smashed
¼ tsp. salt
½ tsp. Mild Hatch Red Chili Powder

Preheat a cast iron griddle in a 375 degree oven. Brush with grapeseed oil, place trout filets on hot griddle, sprinkle with salt and chili powder. Turn on broiler and broil fish on top rack until golden brown, approximately 5 minutes. Combine pecans, butter, and juniper berries. Pour over filets, turn off broiler and keep hot in oven for additional 5 minutes. Garnish with parsley sprigs or cilantro leaves and serve immediately on hot griddle with a side of Panned Corn.

PANNED CORN

 2 ears fresh white or golden corn
 1 tsp. salt
 2 tsp. light brown sugar
 ¼ tsp. Mild Hatch Red Chili Powder
 4 tbsp. vegetable oil or butter

Cut corn from cob and scrape cob to include all the corn milk. Add salt, sugar, chili powder. Heat oil or butter, sauté mixture for 8-10 minutes until cooked.

SEDONA QUAIL WITH WILD MUSHROOM SAUCE ON POTATO CAKE

4 quail with backbone removed, split and flattened
1 c. flour
½ tsp. Mild Hatch Red Chili Powder
¼ tsp. salt
¼ tsp. black pepper
½ c grapeseed oil

In cast iron skill, heat grapeseed oil to 375 degrees. Combine flour, chili powder, salt, and pepper. Dredge quail in flour mixture coating all sides. Shake off excess. Brown quail in oil until golden brown on both sides. Remove to a heated serving platter and place in a 200 degree oven until ready to serve. To serve, place a Potato Cake on heated plate, place quail on top, and spoon Wild Mushroom Sauce over. Garnish with fresh parsley.

WILD MUSHROOM SAUCE

8 oz. fresh wild or baby porcini mushrooms, sliced

1 clove garlic, minced

2 tbsp. shallot, minced

1 tbsp. olive oil

¼ c. dry white wine

3 tbsp. butter

3 tbsp. flour

1 ½ c. light cream

In sauté pan, heat olive oil, add mushrooms, garlic, and shallots and sauté until all liquid is gone and mushrooms are golden. Add wine and reduce gently for 5 minutes. Set aside.

In another pan, melt butter until bubbling, whisk in flour, and cook, stirring constantly, for 5 minutes, being careful not to let mixture burn. Whisk in light cream and stir until mixture is smooth and thickened. Add mushroom mixture, adjust seasoning.

POTATO CAKE

   3 c. peeled, grated raw Yukon Gold potatoes
   1 c. peeled, grated raw purple Peruvian potatoes
   ½ c. white onion, minced
   1 green onion, minced
   1 tbsp. parsley, mince
   ¾ tsp. salt
   ¼ tsp. pepper
   1 tbsp. matzos meal
   1 tbsp. flour
   1 tsp. baking powder
   1 egg
   Vegetable oil for frying

Lightly rinse and squeeze off moisture from grated potatoes. Combine well with all other ingredients, except oil, and refrigerate for 15 minutes. Heat oil in skillet, and spoon in potato mixture to form 4" diameter cakes. Fry, turning once, until golden brown and crisp. Drain on paper towel, and keep warm in 200 degree oven until ready to serve.

CHOCOLATE CHILI POTS
   ½ c. white or raw sugar
   4 tbsp. cocoa powder
   ¼ c. cornstarch
   ¼ c. strong expresso
   1/8 tsp. salt
   2 tsp. pure Hatch red chili powder
   2 ¾ c. milk
   2 tbsp. butter
   1 tsp. vanilla

Mix together dry ingredients. Whisk in milk. Cook over medium heat until mixture coats spoon. Remove from heat, stir in butter and vanilla.

The Author

Resa Milan began recording her recipes from the *Weathervane Café* at the request of her grown children. Later she decided to add a few paragraphs to explain the origin. These paragraphs grew into a light-hearted tale based on the true story that is intended to entertain and amuse.

She still works in the fight against breast cancer and shares her time between Sedona and Myrtle Beach. Look forward to a collection of humerous medical incidents in the future.

To blog both Resa and Barry, and also purchase
the Weathervane Art by Gerry Hoover, go to:

CoffeeontheRockstheNovel.com
Resa@ CoffeeontheRockstheNovel.com

Barry@CoffeontheRockstheNovel.com

CPSIA information can be obtained
at www.ICGtesting.com
Printed in the USA
FFHW020622130719
53608865-59297FF